THE INSIDE STORY
of
STEEL WAGES AND PRICES
1959–1967

THE INSIDE STORY
of
STEEL WAGES AND PRICES
1959–1967

By GEORGE J. MCMANUS

CHILTON BOOK COMPANY
Philadelphia   New York   London

CONTENTS

Intervention Was Obvious 1
An Old Refrain 8
1961 • A New Frontier 24
1962 • The Trap Is Sprung 32
1962 • The Confrontation 44
1962 • The Backwash 57
1962 • Picking Up the Pieces 73
1963 • The Road Back 81
1964 • Almost Perfect 100
1964 • The Bomb 117
1965 • A Preposterous Assembly 136
1965 • A Nice Guidepost Figure 183
1966 • Sure, We Talked to Them 195
There Isn't Much You Can Do 210

THE INSIDE STORY
of
STEEL WAGES AND PRICES
1959–1967

INTERVENTION WAS OBVIOUS

The Secretary of Labor was staggering.

Willard Wirtz had come to the 1965 steel labor negotiations directly from long hours in maritime talks. He was pressed into service as an intermediary. As talks dragged on at the White House, he neared the point of physical collapse. He had lost all capacity to retain information. He kept asking bargainers to repeat things over and over. When eventually they began writing points down on paper, Wirtz had trouble keeping track of the papers. "If ever I saw a man who was inviting a heart attack, it was Willard Wirtz," said a union man later.

Others were starting to show signs of wear and tear. The chief bargainer for the steel companies had developed a stammer. R. Conrad Cooper normally speaks in slow but incisive tones. After nearly 9 months of talks in Pittsburgh and a week of extended Washington sessions, he was having trouble getting his words out.

Only President Johnson seemed unruffled and untired. Without seeming to extend himself, the President rode herd on negotiations, peppering the two sides with statistics, reminding them of the dire consequences of a strike, and making clear by his words and his bearing that a peaceful settlement was absolutely inevitable.

The President began zeroing in on talks August 25 at his press conference. "The decisions which will be made in Pittsburgh this week are of vital importance to everyone in this country and to people in other parts of the world." The President also repeated his specifications for an agreement. "There must be continued cost and price stability in our American economy and I expect full and complete responsibility in current wage negotiations and I expect continued stability in steel prices."

That same day in Pittsburgh, steel management was letting it be known it had done all it could. The companies said they had offered a package costing 40.6¢ an hour over 3 years. That amounted to 3 per cent a year, they said. "The burden of what follows is on the union," warned R. Conrad Cooper, top bargainer and executive vice-president, personnel services, United States Steel Corp.

It seemed the burden had been shifted to the Administration. In early May, a 3 per cent steel settlement had been recommended by the President's Council of Economic Advisers. At the time, this split bargaining positions very neatly down the middle. The companies were offering 2 per cent, while demands of United Steelworkers of America were about 50¢ or 4 per cent. After negotiation, however, the companies had come up to 3 per cent. It appeared that the Administration either had to force the union to accept this wage offer or stand aside for price increases by the companies. A clear test of wage-price guidelines was finally at hand.

If the President was worried, however, he needn't have been. The illusion of clarity was quickly shattered by I. W. Abel, Steelworkers president. The companies were not offering 40.6¢, said Abel; they were offering 37.1¢. This

2

was not for 35 months but for 39 months. "Their latest proposal averages no more than 2.3 per cent of employment costs. . . ." As if that weren't enough, the companies wanted to cut incentives, restrict vacations, and "sweep under the rug many unresolved contract and local issues."

"It appears plainly," said Abel, "that the industry is determined to force a strike." Cooper called the union's estimates "a pea and shell game." Abel said the companies' approach "juggles figures and effective dates, inflates costs and demands concessions . . . which are wholly ridiculous."

The next day—Thursday—both men talked on the phone with President Johnson in Washington. The President again advised that he wanted complete responsibility in the wage negotiations and continued stability in steel prices. Abel and Cooper wished Mr. Johnson a happy birthday. The President, who was 57 on August 27, said he would be happy "if they reached a settlement." They said they would try to be helpful.

Later that day Abel and Cooper met for more than 2 hours with William Simkin, the federal mediator. On Friday, Simkin called the President and said it was no go— the two sides were getting nowhere. Mr. Johnson dispatched two special envoys—Senator Wayne Morse (D., Ore.) and Under Secretary of Commerce LeRoy Collins.

These two arrived in Pittsburgh on Saturday, August 28. Amid a clatter of flashbulbs, they strode purposefully into Pittsburgh's Penn Sheraton Hotel. "My optimism accelerates in any situation I'm involved in," said Morse. The word was that they had flown in with the settlement terms. Reporters set up a full-time watch to cover the meetings in Simkin's hotel suite and in U. S. Steel's offices down the street. There were reports that Cooper was sweetening the pie and that the union had come down from 50¢. Throughout Saturday there was a sense of impending ac-

3

tion and reporters were clocking meetings and sending out minute-by-minute accounts of all movements.

By Sunday, the edge had worn off. News people were still camped outside Simkin's door, but they no longer had their pencils poised. The official view now held that the special representatives had been sent to "isolate" the issues. On Sunday, President Johnson received a "lengthy" report from his troubleshooters. There had been no progress, said the President that afternoon in a news conference at his Texas home.

What was he going to do now? "I'm going to avoid a walkout." But suppose the deadlock continued? The government had to "take one step at a time." If there isn't a settlement, "we'll have to look to the national interest and see what it requires and carry it out." The President wasn't asked if he would seek a Taft-Hartley injunction. He very carefully avoided any kind of specific threat of intervention. Nevertheless, the papers jumped on his words and headlined the warning of intervention.

In Pittsburgh, there was a final brief meeting Sunday night in the U. S. Steel building of top negotiators and the government officials. Wayne Morse stomped out in a grumpy mood. The deadlock was "inexcusable and unjustifiable. I think they are making a great mistake in not reaching an agreement." Secretary Collins, who did not seem too deeply involved, was a little more hopeful. He said there was no sign of bitterness and talks were continuing. With this, Morse and Collins flew back to Washington, leaving things no worse than when they had arrived.

They had breakfast with President Johnson on Monday. An hour later came the move experts had been predicting for 9 months. The negotiators were summoned to Washington.

The President sent his own plane to fetch the bargainers. The union team accepted the ride, but company negotiators

4

said they would fly separately. In response to management's declining, Secretary of Commerce John T. Connor called Pittsburgh and said Mr. Johnson would be unhappy. This made the company officials unhappy. They flew to Washington in their own plane but when they arrived they were collected by Marines and, together with the union delegation, were lifted by helicopter to the White House.

At the White House, Mr. Johnson seated his guests in the Cabinet room. "The President spoke with us for about 45 minutes," said R. Conrad Cooper. "In the words of Isaiah, it was suggested that we reason together." "He reviewed the nation's present defense needs," said the union, "and he reviewed the state of the economy as a whole." The White House said the President made a "strong, unemotional appeal to put the national interest first." He read a CEA report spelling out the "tragic consequences" of a strike for the economy. He said the Department of Defense had advised it could not afford the loss of a single day's steel production.

After this, Mr. Johnson and Secretary Wirtz had lunch with the union group. Secretary of Commerce Connor dined with the company people. In most subsequent sessions, this alignment was followed: Wirtz worked with the union and Connor with the companies. CEA Chairman Gardner Ackley devoted himself "full time to an attempt to narrow the disputed items." Ackley was described as sort of a statistical referee.

At 3 P.M., actual talks began. By about 8 P.M. or earlier, an agreement on an 8-day extension had been negotiated. At this point, there was a delay of an hour or so while arrangements were being made for TV time. The President left with Cooper and Abel. The other company and union people were told to sit tight until the television announcement.

This caused great anguish in the company delegation. It

5

was then August 30, only 24 hours before the strike deadline. The companies were beginning to bank blast furnaces and seal open hearths. U. S. Steel figured it took 2 days to make a complete shutdown and about 10 days to get things going afterwards. With mills going down, company bargainers were cut off from the outside world. During the waiting period, they moaned that the delay was costing them "millions." (Afterwards, it turned out there was only a minor production loss.)

This was really the only time anything close to physical duress was applied to the bargainers. There was a certain amount of joshing about Marines with bayonets standing over the steel people but it was never quite that bad.

The union officials were actually a little put out at the lack of attention they received after working hours. Following the extension announcement and a late bargaining session Monday night, the Steelworkers delegation was dumped out on the streets of Washington and left to fend for itself. During their week in Washington, Abel and his associates walked the 2 or 3 blocks from the White House to the Statler Hotel each day. They were open targets for reporters but didn't even get much of a play from them. The company bargainers stayed at the Carlton Hotel. On hand at the hotel were the chief executives of the major steel companies. Roger Blough and the other leaders remained in the background during Washington talks. Cooper and the other bargainers rode to and from the White House in a U. S. Steel Corp. car. "They didn't smile all week," said a chauffeur.

It was not surprising the steel people didn't smile that week in Washington. For years, they had worked to get their wage and price problems out of the public spotlight. They had tried to find some way of negotiating wages in an orderly, private, moderate manner. They had tried to prove that steel was not a strike-happy industry—that it

6

could settle labor matters without the help of the federal government. Likewise, the industry had argued it was not a grasping monopoly. It was not always raising prices in lock step. It should not be subjected to unending scrutiny and badgering in price decisions.

On both counts—wages and prices—the industry had been doing well. In 1962 and again in 1963, it had negotiated peaceful settlements with the steel union. In both years, agreements came months before a possible strike deadline. Moreover, moderate labor terms had been matched by price moderation. From 1958 through 1965, there had been only one significant price increase. Increases in the 7-year period had been largely offset by reductions. It seemed that the mills were well on the way to demonstrating they could manage wages and prices without the advice and consent of the federal government.

Yet here, in September of 1965, the steel men were in Washington again. They were being told in very specific terms what to do about wages and what to do about prices.

How did it all happen? After the fine record of recent years, why did the chief steel negotiator have to admit that federal intervention in 1965 was "obvious"? What chain of events led many authorities to predict months before that the 1965 negotiations would be settled by Lyndon Johnson? And where was this chain reaction leading?

AN OLD REFRAIN

When the new nations of the world reach out for progress, one of the first things they want is a steel mill. Steel is a symbol. It is the foundation material of the industrial age. The amount of steel used is still a measure of how fast a nation is adding to the machines that raise living standards. But the importance of steel as a symbol and a barometer goes beyond any statistical evaluation. In this country, anyway, steelmaking has been a focal point in the process of reconciling free, individual enterprise with an age of big companies, big unions, big machines, and big government.

For much of the postwar period, this process was marked by constant action but no fundamental change. In each episode, the tide would change just when it seemed there would be some final resolution.

The 1961 sequence began with steel management picking up a familiar refrain. This time, however, there was to be no turning back. A buildup of words and acts would carry principals to a full, decisive collision. On May 10, 1961, Thomas F. Patton spoke at the annual meeting of Republic

Steel Corp. President of Republic, Patton said his company could not maintain "reasonable profits unless there is some compensating price increase." On May 24, a very similar statement came from Avery C. Adams, chairman, Jones & Laughlin Steel Corp. No industry would keep increasing labor costs "without either a compensating price increase or inadequate profits." Arthur B. Homer, chairman of Bethlehem Steel Corp. warned, "There will be a time when things come to a head."

Before these comments, quite a few things had happened. Many years before, the earth's crust had solidified with an iron content of 4 or 5 per cent. Three thousand years ago, men learned that iron ore, which is in oxide form, could be reduced by heating it in the presence of some carbon-bearing material.

Also very early, it was learned that pure iron, which is relatively soft, could be strengthened by adding a pinch of carbon. Steel is defined as an alloy of iron and carbon, containing no more than 1.7 per cent carbon. At elevated temperatures, up to 1.7 per cent carbon will dissolve in the spaces between the iron atoms. When the metal cools, the iron atoms rearrange themselves and the carbon is precipitated out in patterns that can give an infinite variety of properties.

In modern practice, iron ore is melted and reduced in blast furnaces that use coke as the carbon source. Blast furnace iron has about 4 per cent carbon. This is refined to steel in open hearths or oxygen vessels by burning off the carbon with air or pure oxygen.

Steel is very strong. In its mildest, low-carbon form it will withstand a pressure of 25,000 pounds a square inch without yielding. It will also take a lot of heat; refining temperatures are close to 3000° Fahrenheit.

Steelmaking has a long maturing process behind it. American mills turned out 3.3 million ingot tons in 1887.

9

That was more than the 2.7 million tons of primary aluminum made in 1965. In recent years, U. S. mills have been producing more than 130 million ingot tons and users have been chewing up 100 million tons of finished product.

The American steel industry has been shaped by all these factors—the nature of the metal, its strength and usefulness; its wide acceptance, and its long period of market and technical development.

These factors have resulted in the following characteristics of the industry:

1. Steel is made by big companies in big plants. Years of tonnage operation have produced a buildup of equipment size and a refinement of technology. The tendency is to get improvement by making machines bigger and faster. It takes enormous expenditures today to get modest improvements. To build an efficient new mill now, say steel engineers, you must figure on a capacity of 3 million tons and a cost of more than 1 billion dollars.

2. Steel products and processes are highly standardized. For mass production efficiency at the mill and in the fabricating plant, there must be a certain degree of sameness. Ninety per cent of all tonnage is carbon steel—its properties are determined primarily by carbon and iron. Most steel is produced to industry-wide specifications.

3. Steel prices are based on mass production efficiency, developed, again, over more than 50 years. The average steel product sells for $150 to $160 a ton. Aluminum is three or four times more expensive by weight. Aluminum is just now going through the transition from job shop production to mass production while steel made this switch long ago.

4. Steel is not, or was not, subject to price-volume elasticity in a positive way. It has already made the maximum penetration in many markets. Nearly 2 tons of steel go into the manufacture of the average auto. In the first

10

6 months of 1966, 1.9 million tons of steel went into cans from a total metal use of 2 million tons. The steel industry might lose business by increasing prices but it has, or had, no positive incentive to make price cuts.

There are other things. Steelmaking is a violent operation. The word *steel* has connotations of unyielding, deadly hardness. The early labor history, from the Homestead battle in 1891 to the Memorial Day shooting in 1937, was turbulent. Some of the history and character of the thing clings to men who now make steel. The industry is trying to reshape its image along lighter and brighter lines but there is still a special drama in any steel crisis.

There is also a special overtone to any steel price move. Since the days when Judge Gary was promoting fraternal feelings through his dinners, there has always been the suggestion of an evil, monopolistic plot. Price increases— in strong markets or weak—supposedly have reflected a lack of competition. At the same time, the biggest steel companies have known that if they competed effectively enough to eliminate smaller companies, they would be attacked for monopolistic tendencies.

Nothing that happened in the early postwar years did anything to get the steel industry out of the limelight or off the spot. There were strikes in 1946, 1948, 1952, 1955, and 1956. Three of these shutdowns involved full-scale tilts with the government under President Harry Truman. In 1952, the steel industry was seized by the government. In both 1946 and 1952, steel prices were formally involved in disputes. From 1940 to 1958, steel prices rose more than 170 per cent. Federal probers hammered away at this record. Steel is a monopolistic trust that milks the economy, they said. The steel answer was simple. Prices rose because labor costs were pushed up in an arbitrary, regular fashion. Steel employment costs climbed more than 300 per cent in the 20 years after 1940.

In 1958, both the wage and the price trends reached some sort of climax. The steel market was in a dismal state. Production of 85 million ingot tons was the lowest since 1947. At the same time, the mills were due to be hit in July with one of their biggest postwar pay hikes—20¢ an hour.

This was the setting in June of 1958. Everyone was speculating on the amount of the price hike that would automatically follow the wage boost. Senator Estes Kefauver was agitating against the increase.

At this point, U. S. Steel came out with a curious statement. Prices were determined by a great range of competitive and cost factors, it said; there was some question as to when these factors would add up to a price increase. It added: "It must be obvious to anyone that the matter of price adjustment would not even come up under present circumstances if it were not for the very substantial employment cost increase we now face."

The popular interpretation was that U. S. Steel was putting out the word that someone else would have to carry the ball this time—it was not going to be the price leader. But whatever was intended, the only result of the statement was to defer price action a month or so. In late July, Armco Steel Corp. led off with an increase in sheet steel. Others followed and threw in their own products. A general increase, averaging $4.50 a ton, went through.

One account of the 1962 crisis recalled that Armco had "revolted" against U. S. Steel in 1958. This seems a fairly innocent view. Whatever the true meaning of the June statement, it's difficult to imagine U. S. Steel finding anything revolting in a steel price increase. And it is a fact that U. S. Steel went along with the others.

Anyway, steel prices did go up in the middle of a horrible market slump. According to the antitrusters, this action defied the law of supply and demand. It provided ammunition in 1961 for demanding advance action against a steel increase in another period of weak demand. Steel management could argue labor costs were also resisting the pressure of supply and demand. It could also be argued that steel is a mass production industry with heavy capital costs. At the same time, it is a cyclical industry, subject to big market swings. Because mills provided enough capacity for peak periods, they had heavy capital charges in periods of low demand.

If the industry did not do this—if it did not provide the funds for carrying idle capacity in lean periods—the cost to consumers would ultimately be much greater. Copper users, for example, find prices going through the ceiling in the recurring shortages. Steel men note in this connection that they never auction their products off in boom markets.

But apart from long-range philosophy, the practical question in 1958 was simple enough for steel men. Five mills had lost money in the first half. The whole industry was operating near the break-even point. How could a huge wage package be absorbed without price relief?

In 1959, management proposed that the existing labor contract be extended 1 year with no change in pay. The cost of living clause was to be dropped under this proposal.

It was a now-or-never situation for the tough school of management. The 1958 sequence had shown the damaging effects of aggressive labor and soft management. There was a Republican in the White House and there probably wouldn't be the next time around. Also, steel users had ample opportunity to put in extra inventory for the strike stand. Steel stocks were increased by 10 to 12 million tons in the first half of 1959.

In this situation, the mills made their pitch for a wage hold-down. Heading the industry's team for the first time was R. Conrad Cooper, a lean, stern man, who had played football at Minnesota and once considered professional

13

boxing as a career. Cooper replaced John A. Stephens, a poised gentleman, who could listen to union tirades without flinching.

Cooper is the strong, silent type. He looks like a man to be reckoned with in any situation, a man of inner reserves and controlled power. His personal force does not come through in photographs or television appearances, but at close range he is an impressive person. Once he backed another reporter and myself against the wall in a hotel corridor. He demanded to know if either of us had called him at home at 1 A.M. the previous morning. We hadn't but it was still a baleful moment.

Cooper has not hesitated to show his impatience with anything he considers a digression from practical issues. "Oh, quit it," he said once in response to questions on the philosophy behind new union programs. "We've said what we'd give." He can be brusque. His rejections of 1965 union proposals were quick and unequivocal. "Preposterous," he said of one union package. He has made some powerful public statements, but more often than not his official pronouncements are heavy and ponderous. A spectator gets the impression of a cold, hard, ramrod of a man. This picture breaks down when you talk to union negotiators. "He's a fine gentleman," says Joe Molony, Steelworkers vice-president. "Coop's a fine gentleman," says Marvin Miller, the brilliant staff worker who has since become the representative of baseball players. One close associate strenuously objects to the characterization of Cooper as an unfeeling, unyielding person. "He's a man of granite— there's no question about that—but it's that inner strength that permits him to be generous." On the basis of kindness and fairness, as well as strength, "he stands 10 feet tall."

Union people minimize personal problems. They represent Cooper as the unfortunate head of an unwieldy bargaining apparatus, the servant of many masters and the

14

executor of impossible policies. It's a little difficult to see Cooper as a meek figurehead, and in 1959 certainly, the second part of the management platform could have originated with him and his industrial engineering background.

This second section involved a series of demands for elimination of various worker abuses. The industry proposed tougher penalties against wildcat strikes and slowdowns. It demanded clear acceptance of management's right to develop incentives and establish sound practices. It sought clarification of scheduling rights. The whole push revolved around a proposal that sounded harmless enough. The companies wanted to "modify ambiguous and restrictive language so as to enable management to make operating improvements in the interest of greater efficiency and economy." This centered on contract paragraph 2B, which stated that a past practice could not be changed without a change in the basic work situation.

This formal past practice provision had been added to contracts at the request of the companies. The idea had been to set a cutoff for establishing a new local practice.

However, the language was worked out in the bleary hours of the morning, in the rush before a settlement, and as a result of unclear wording, the paragraph only had the effect of giving official status to a doctrine that was detrimental to the interests of management. A mill could install a major facility and determine how many operators should be assigned. But management could not go into a department where three people were working and decide only two were needed—not without a lot of fuss, anyway.

The industry's position was explained at the time by R. Heath Larry, a vice-president of U. S. Steel who served with Cooper on the industry barganing committee: "We found after adoption of the past-practice provision that the union kept pushing the idea that everything had to be the way it has always been. When a man finds a way to improve conditions, he knows the union will probably oppose the change. He cannot get a clear or certain answer to how arbitrators will interpret contract language for his proposal. There is an intangible here—a frustration. We can't precisely measure how much this feeling slows progress but we do see a danger that management, as well as labor, could settle into frozen attitudes."

That was one of management's problems in negotiating —it couldn't measure the extent of the problem. It came up with only a few examples of abuses. The lack of documentation was a puzzling weakness in the industry's case. There was featherbedding in the mills. Anyone with a casual acquaintance of the industry knew of cases in which men were being payed too much or doing too little. One U. S. Steel supervisor cited a case in which a relative of a union official was drawing a check for sitting in a corner and doing nothing. The man couldn't be fired and he couldn't handle the work available. This particular supervisor came from a union family; his father was still working in the open hearth. He said it was not a black-and-white situation but that there was considerable justice to management's claim of widespread inefficiency.

Whether featherbedding was worse than in other industries or worse than in management may have been a question but there is no doubt that the companies' reticence on this point may have stemmed from the belated realization that it might not be too smart to cite hundreds of situations in which men would be fired if the companies got the power they were seeking.

Even without specific illustration, however, this message did register on the rank and file. Men would be thrown out of work if the companies won. "We didn't even have to tell them," said the USWA staff man. "The companies did it for us."

Before the question of job reforms arose, an opinion sur-

16

vey showed steelworkers strongly opposed to a strike. Many authorities believe the most nominal terms would have been accepted by the union at this stage. *Iron Age* publisher Tom Campbell says the union at one stage had indicated through go-betweens it would settle for something like 10¢ an hour. Campbell says the way had been paved on both sides for a settlement along these lines but that the more hawklike management faction held out for total victory. The job reform program solidified the union. After the list of reforms was published, another opinion survey showed the workers ready to go down the line in resistance to management's proposals.

There was talk then and later that the industry had made an unrealistic blunder in raising the efficiency issue. For one thing, said an official of General Electric Co., you can't settle local problems in national bargaining.

The steel industry certainly did not settle anything in 1959. After a 2-week extension at the request of President Eisenhower, a strike began in the middle of July. The President had offered some soothing counsel earlier but it was clear he intended to let free collective bargaining run its course. The shutdown dragged on through July, August, and September with a lot of public haranguing, but little progress resulted and there was no move by the Administration. It was evident that steel users had stocked up for a long siege; there was remarkably little change in industrial production as the strike continued through 30 and 60 days.

Not until late October and early November did the economy begin grinding to a standstill. With auto plants and others announcing shutdowns, the President finally started the Taft-Hartley proceedings for an 80-day cooling-off period.

The Steelworkers opposed the injunction, and the union's counsel, Arthur Goldberg, argued the case very ably in

17

federal courts. "Strikes are not a failure of collective bargaining," said Goldberg. "They are a part of collective bargaining." A variation of this thought had been stated in 1949 by Charles M. White, chief executive of Republic Steel, in hearings of a fact-finding board. "If they think we're wrong, they strike us. See? That's the way this thing should work. It's a hell of a good way." In 1965, I. W. Abel was quoted as saying that "there are worse things than strikes." All these remarks, unfortunately, center on what seems to be an essential truth: free collective bargaining involves the freedom to strike.

There may be some middle ground but it hasn't been found yet. In Canada, where the law provides lengthy mediation before a shutdown, there is often no serious bargaining until legal formalities have been completed and an effective strike threat exists. In the United States, when the government has indicated it will go beyond mediation, the tendency has been for bargainers to rest on their oars and protect positions.

In 1959, the Eisenhower Administration allowed the free process to be carried to its ultimate, bitter end, and after 116 days of tragic waste, nothing had been settled.

When the injunction took effect, the mills quickly got their furnaces going. In addition, they stepped up their communications bombardment of employees and the public. Countless brochures stated management's case. During the whole dispute, some 20 advertisements were run in 400 newspapers. As far as worker reaction went, this effort was a failure. The Taft-Hartley Law says that after 60 days of the cooling-off period, workers shall vote on the last offer of the companies.

Before the official ballot, the companies made an informal check and found workers strongly opposed to the offer and firmly united in support of the union. This response may have convinced management of the futility of further battling. Heading off public disavowal by their employees, the companies signed a contract that gave the union 40¢ an hour over 3 years and contained none of management's job reforms.

The industry consoled itself that the 3.5 per cent package was at least a break from the postwar average of 8 per cent a year. At the time, however, it looked as though the 1959 adventure had ended in a complete and crushing defeat for management. Moreover, the metalworking economy never got going again after the strike. A report prepared for the Department of Commerce in 1961 minimized the effect of the shutdown but it is a fact that business went into a tailspin in early 1960. The mills enjoyed a few brisk months while users were rebuilding inventories, but by the end of the first quarter, demand was sinking rapidly.

Another unhappy development for steel people was the influx of foreign metal. One argument for the 1959 stand was the need to stabilize costs so American mills could compete with overseas suppliers. The union tended to regard this as only a talking point and, until 1959, imports were negligible. However, the strike opened the door. Steel imports jumped from 2 million tons in 1958 to 5 million tons in 1959. Imports dropped again in 1960, but they never returned to the 1958 level. The foothold gained during the strike was steadily expanded.

It was difficult at the time to see any good coming out of the 1959 shutdown, yet later events suggest there may have been both tangible and intangible benefits. At Kaiser Steel Corp., a long-range committee was set up to seek better solutions to labor problems. Labor, management, and the public were represented on the committee. At Pittsburgh Steel Co., a grass-roots program showed that the communications barrier between management and workers could be overcome. Instead of relying on canned verbiage, Pittsburgh Steel officials went out to the homes and communities of the workers. They presented company problems in candid, adult terms. Although the company's proposals were defeated in the industry's only Taft-Hartley vote one-third of the workers did side with the company in a program calling for pay cuts for 20 per cent of all employees. Pittsburgh Steel was later able to negotiate a plan for correcting excessive incentive rates. The whole industry at least had the satisfaction of fighting for what it considered right. For years, management people had been damning the union in private bars and giving in when the test came.

The 1959 experience may have purged frustrations on both sides. It provided a demonstration of will that was possibly important in later negotiations. "Our problem in 1959," said one staff man, "was that after years of backing down, we couldn't convince the union we meant what we said."

The business of establishing credibility is cited by union people when they are asked how workers will ever make up the money lost in a strike. The payoff, say union men, comes in later years because management knows the strike threat is not a bluff.

There is no question that the memory of the 1959 strike played a part in the modest steel settlements of 1962 and 1963. On both sides, there was a reaction away from strife and toward harmony.

The agreement also provided a vehicle for achieving better feeling—the Human Relations Committee. This group was to meet on a continuing basis to study problems and come up with facts.

Previous agreements had called for committee activity on job classification and incentives. Nothing much had been accomplished. Many veterans regarded the Human Relations program and the Kaiser program as nice-sounding efforts that would wither away. "If there is the will for agreement, you can get an agreement in a week," said a steel vice-president. "If there is not the right feeling, no amount of talk is going to change anything." The Human Relations Committee, however, did start talking in April of 1960, with the participants still bitter and bruised.

Other things were happening in 1960. John F. Kennedy, running on a program of action, was elected by a slender margin. His great commitment was to do things that would get the country going. An inconspicuous plank in the Democratic platform called for action against increases of administered prices.

One thing did not happen in 1960: steel prices did not go up. The industry took no action in the first half of the year although benefits estimated at 14¢ an hour took effect January 1.

This was the first time in the memory of purchasing agents that a cost hike was not passed along. The omission caused no great stir in the excitement of the settlement but many dopesters later charged political motives. The theory was that Richard Nixon, who had helped work out the 1959 settlement, extracted a promise that steel prices would not be increased that year. Supposedly, a hike would have reflected on the Republican Administration and on Nixon's bid for the presidency. U. S. Steel chairman, Roger Blough, later denied politics had anything to do with the timing of price moves. "I wouldn't even know how to operate in that area," he said. Without any partisan commitment, Blough and others may have been fearful of projecting steel prices into the charged atmosphere of a presidential year.

Apart from this, 1960 was a period of bad business and general price weakness. Steel operations, after the inventory flurry, sank to about 50 per cent of capacity. The whole industrial economy was caught in a profit squeeze. In the first half of the year, Aluminum Co. of America

21

reported an $8 million drop in earnings despite a $20 million sales gain. Equipment makers and others reported deep price cuts. "Price levels are not in keeping with the volume of business being done," said G. G. Beard, President, United Engineering & Foundry Co. A purchasing agent noted the weakness of ferroalloy prices. "They pushed the panic button. There was no sense to the kind of price cuts they put through."

There was no question that industry, which had been told to prepare for the soaring sixties, was having trouble adjusting to the prolonged period of soft demand and excess of supply.

One possible factor was the crackdown on price-fixing. The lurid cases in the electrical industry had shocked the public. In these and a few others, businessmen had been sent to jail for price conspiracy for the first time in history. By September of 1960, the Department of Justice had filed 58 collusion cases. The Federal Trade Commission had issued 130 price discrimination complaints—nearly double the 1959 total. "Despite the dramatic increase," said FTC chairman, Earl W. Kinter, "it seems clear to me that we have only scratched the surface."

In short, the commercial and political climate was not favorable for price increases. And steel people were becoming more and more worried about imports. "We sure saw some tough competition," said R. W. Simon, chief metallurgical engineer, U. S. Steel, after a tour of European sheet mills. Foreign plants were now equipped with the most modern facilities, said W. H. Mayo, manager of process control metallurgy for U. S. Steel. "You'd think you were right at home when you look at their newer mills," said Mr. Mayo.

All this probably influenced steel people more than any deal with Nixon. If there had been a specific deal, it's difficult to understand why the mills did not boost prices in

December of 1960, when the Republicans had lost their election and labor costs were going up another 11¢ or so.

Looking back, that was the last time the industry had a clear shot at price increases. If they had known what was coming, the mills might have put through a whopper of a hike. Maybe not, though.

1961 · A NEW FRONTIER

The Administration had promised it would do things. The Nation had stagnated under Republicans, it said. The new frontiersmen would act. They would not just let things happen. They would intervene and direct and move. For the first time, steel wage and price moves would draw not isolated reactions but a planned, consistent response.

When the new Administration took office in 1961, it was rapidly made clear wages and prices were a prime concern. Arthur Goldberg, now Secretary of Labor, jumped into a New York tugboat strike and brought a settlement. A month later, Mr. Goldberg settled a dispute of flight engineers. In May, no-srike, no-lockout pledges were secured from missile-site contractors and unions. This was the first such agreement in peacetime history. Arthur Goldberg insisted the Administration was not out to take over collective bargaining. However, he also left no doubt that its role would extend beyond putting out occasional brush fires.

In February, a labor-management advisory committee was established with seven labor leaders, seven business

24

people, and seven representatives of the public. "This is just the beginning," said Goldberg. "The important thing is to make both sides realize they must act out of the public interest and that as the representatives of the public, government must concern itself in the process." On May 16, he called on labor and management to find ways to prevent work stoppages.

It was in this setting that steel people began talking about the need for higher prices. Comments by Patton, Adams, and other steel leaders drew a quick response from the Administration. "I do not think any price increase would be received very well publicly or in the business community," said Secretary of Commerce Luther Hodges. In late May, word was out that the Council of Economic Advisers was beginning an informal study of steel prices.

Business people could sense a tightening noose and tried to assert their independence. Roger Blough was then chairman of the Business Advisory Council, a 60-man group that was apparently supposed to receive advice rather than give it. Blough had succeeded Ralph J. Cordiner, who headed General Electric during the price conspiracy trial. As a result of tightened government supervision, Cordiner resigned in May, 1961, and Blough became chairman.

In July, the council officially proclaimed its status as a nongovernmental body. A letter from Blough cited a Kennedy quote as backing for the move. "We know that your success and ours are intertwined. We seek the spirit of full-fledged alliance." The group changed its name to Business Council. Hodges objected but President Kennedy decided to smile and make the best of things. He said the broadened base was a good idea.

Also in July, Conrad Cooper attacked the Administration's labor policies as leading to "government controls of all major bargaining, a steppingstone to the establishment of national wage and price policies."

All this time, steel people were still talking about price increases but doing a pretty good job of price cutting. Line-pipe prices were reduced $18 a ton in a move that reflected competition from small electric-weld mills. Producers of stainless steel were making official price cuts and were bidding against each other on a day-to-day basis. In May, Allegheny Ludlum Steel Corp. came out with a low-price stainless steel specifically designed for use in automobile mufflers. This horrified some steel men who felt the muffler grade was a step away from the one-price system of the industry and a move toward the commodity pricing that had caused problems in the aluminum industry.

Most steels are priced on a product basis. The aluminum companies have tended to emphasize markets to a greater extent with special prices for can stock, siding sheet, and other applications. Ideally, the prices represent distinct properties and economics. Very often, the commodity system resulted in taking a standard product and cutting the price to get business. "Commodity pricing is entirely logical in theory but look what's happened to aluminum profits," said one stainless producer. "I'm against it in any form."

On June 23, U. S. Steel withdrew its published price for reenforcing bars and said it would negotiate orders in the future. Imports of rebars had moved over 500,000 tons a year, or 14 per cent of domestic supply. The big mills were also feeling the effects of competition from small shops in outlying areas. These actions were typical of what was happening in all industrial markets. "Prices are horrible," said J. B. Dury, Jr., sales manager, Rosedale Foundry & Machine Co. "They're all over the map. On some things, prices are below what they were in 1955." Similar words came from John P. Roche, who was then president of Heppenstall Co. and who is now president of the American Iron and Steel Institute. "We're selling forgings at lower prices than they were five years ago," said Roche. R. W. Ewalt, sales manager of Rust Furnace Co., reported sales volume at its lowest point since 1938.

Electrical equipment was selling for 15 per cent off list. "The pendulum went the other way after the antitrust cases," said one purchasing agent. Earnings of Westinghouse Electric Corp. were down 50 per cent on a sales drop of 2 per cent in the second quarter.

It didn't seem a time for anyone to be worrying about inflation. However, the trustbusters could point to 1958, when steel prices went up at an unlikely time. Also they could note the recent words of steel executives.

On July 3, the importance of steel price cuts was minimized by Logan T. Johnston, president, Armco Steel Corp. Major products had not been affected, Johnston asserted. Tom Patton of Republic was equally reassuring. "Prices on products involving the large percentage of shipments remain firm," said Patton. "The basic factors which make a price increase necessary continue to be very strong and will grow even stronger after the next wage increase next October," he added.

In the light of later events, this might have been an excellent time to say nothing about price hikes and a lot about price cuts. It must be remembered, however, that steel executives had things other than political reactions to think about. They were holding the price line on most products in the face of determined efforts by users to get concessions. If purchasing agents had gotten one mill to backslide a little, they could have started playing companies against each other.

From a commercial standpoint, therefore, it was desirable to discourage talk of weakness and provide reassurance that no one was being quietly undercut. Apart from

27

specific strategy, every financial instinct impels the business executive to dwell on the possibility of price increases and play down price weakness.

Nevertheless, the 1961 steel statements may have triggered a fateful series of events. On August 2, Senator Kefauver indicated his senate subcommittee would start a probe if steel prices rose.

On August 23, Senator Albert Gore (D., Tenn.) urged President Kennedy "to bar a price rise by breaking up large companies to restore competition or to control prices if more persuasion failed."

On August 30, the President, in a press conference, asked that steel prices be kept at current levels. On September 4, the Council of Economic Advisors said the industry could earn good money without higher prices. Steel productivity gains were offsetting wage hikes, said the CEA.

On September 6, President Kennedy made a direct, formal appeal to the industry. In letters to the presidents of 12 major mills, he reviewed the inflationary history of steel wages and prices. He said the industry could make "good profits" without a price hike, and he hinted that the government would lend a hand in getting a moderate labor settlement in 1962. "If the industry were now to forgo a price increase, it would enter collective bargaining negotiations next spring with a record of three and a half years of price stability. It would clearly then be the turn of labor representatives to limit wage demands to a level consistent with continued price stability."

This argument was received without enthusiasm by the industry. Joseph L. Block, chairman of Inland Steel Co., said steel profits were already too low. "However," he said, "if it is deemed in the public interest that prices be frozen, then it would seem to me also in the public interest for employment costs to be frozen for a year." Thomas E. Millsop, chairman of National Steel Corp., saw "very serious questions as to legality as well as business management and economic problems."

On September 13, Roger Blough of U. S. Steel, replied to the President with figures showing the relatively low profits of the industry and the minor impact of steel prices on the economy. Blough pointed out, again, that steel employment costs rose 322 per cent from 1940 to 1958. He argued that the basic idea of government guidance was wrong. The economic advisers, he said, "seem to be assuming the role of informal price setters for steel." "If for steel, what then for automobiles, or rubber or electrical products or food or paper or chemicals. . . . Do we thus head into unworkable, stifling peacetime control of prices?"

For the Steelworkers, David McDonald said the coming wage settlement should give "full weight to the public interest." President Kennedy replied that this would be done by reaching a settlement "within the limits of advances in productivity and price stability."

On September 21, Blough went to the White House. He later said he made it clear that "no one could speak for the industry about prices and that there was no question about the freedom of any company to change prices." * "I felt he was under no misapprehension on this matter although my associates and I believed that competitive conditions precluded a price rise on October 1." ". . . no commitment on price of any kind was made at that September meeting.

Blough, who had come to U. S. Steel from a Wall Street law firm, had laid the groundwork for subsequent actions. In the opinion of some people, however, this only showed that the steel executive was planning a price increase right along. It did not show, say detractors, that Blough had tried to communicate his thinking in clear, unmistakable terms.

* *Look,* January 29, 1963.

Assuming there had been definite price plans at this early date, it nevertheless is possible the whole thing was a simple misunderstanding. When all cards were on the table months later, Blough still had trouble cutting through tangled arguments and getting to the basic guts of the matter. It's also possible no amount of plain talk could have gotten through to an Administration eager to see its design accepted.

When October 1 came and there was no price increase, the Kennedy people chalked up one victory. They had stemmed the inflationary tide. They may or may not have blocked a steel price increase, but there was no general wave of inflation. The fuss over prices seemed inappropriate among other things.

But if the Administration was tilting against a windmill, it was merely responding to a pet obsession of the steel industry. For years, steel leaders had agitated against inflation as the greatest of all evils. The starting points for steel people were government spending and labor demands. It doesn't seem to have occurred to anyone that steel prices would be prime targets in any general push for stability.

At any rate, the Administration thought a deal had been made in the fall of 1961. The companies could have set things straight by raising prices October 1. Or they could have stated their position in elementary English. They could have said: "Look, Charlie, regardless of what you do in the labor business, we're going to raise prices."

At the time, the companies may not have thought there was any real need to shake off a commitment. The Administration had offered a few nice generalities about labor restraint but in management's view, the whole history of intervention suggested the government would give labor what it wanted and then pronounce the settlement fair and noninflationary.

On January 14, 1946, President Harry Truman told basic

steel to accept an 18¢ increase "on the grounds of public interest, as well as good business. . . ." In 1948, President Truman handed the mills a "statesmanlike formula" calling for them to recognize pension demands. On March 20, 1952, the Wage Stabilization Board came up with a 17½¢ package. Prior to this, U. S. Steel had offered to forgo a price increase if the union would defer wage demands.

When the companies balked at the wage proposal, Truman really landed on them. "The companies have said, in short, that unless they have what they want, the steel industry will shut down. They not only want to raise their prices to cover any wage increases; they want to double their money in the deal." The President then directed Secretary of Commerce Sawyer to seize the steel industry. Federal Judge David A. Pine overturned the seizure on April 29. The whole incident left steel men firmly convinced that government intervention would only be on a flagrantly partisan basis.

The outlook in late 1961 seemed particularly unfavorable for management. Not only was there a Democratic Administration but the Secretary of Labor, Arthur Goldberg, had been counsel for the Steelworkers. Nevertheless, the Administration continued to talk in serious tones about labor rates. On October 2, 1961, Arthur Goldberg declared that the government would "speak with equal clarity" on wages. In November and December, Goldberg contacted steel bargainers to urge an early, noninflationary settlement. He offered the help of the Administration.

In December, Goldberg gave the word to delegates at the AFL–CIO convention in Miami. The Administration did not have a rigid wage policy but "wage increases should be earned by productivity." Goldberg talked to Dave McDonald in Florida about early negotiation. He spoke also to the top company bargainer, R. Conrad Cooper.

1962 · THE TRAP IS SPRUNG

It's almost certain historians will regard 1962 as a year in which a decisive change took place in the American system of free, private enterprise. A new doctrine of economic management by government was asserted. This doctrine was applied. It was challenged. The confrontation that followed produced an authentic change in the role of government and in the rules for business operation.

Until the start of 1962, this "doctrine" had been expressed largely in generalities. It was all very good to talk about productivity, but steel people remembered 1946 and 1952 when demands they considered outrageous had been handed them by the government. In January, 1962, the Administration began getting specific. The President's Council of Economic Advisers came out with its famous wage-price guideline. Contained in the CEA's annual report, the key guideline principles were simple enough:

1. "Individual wage and price decisions assume national importance when they involve large numbers of workers and large amounts of output . . . there is a legitimate

reason for public interest in their content and consequences.

2. "An informed public . . . can help create an atmosphere in which the parties to such decisions will exercise their powers responsibly.

3. "The general guide for non-inflationary wage behavior is that the rate of increase in wage rates in each industry be equal to the trend rate of overall productivity increase.

4. "The general guide for non-inflationary price behavior calls for price reduction if the industry's rate of productivity increase exceeds the overall rate . . . it calls for an appropriate increase in price if the opposite relationship prevails."

The Council presented these tenets in a diffident, almost offhand, manner. It emphasized that formal wage-price controls were "neither desirable . . . nor practical." There could be "no simple test" for wage-price decisions. The Council's thesis was intended as a "contribution to . . . discussion."

Most important, perhaps, the CEA noted that it was almost impossible to measure productivity—the central element in the package. It came to be accepted that 3.2 per cent was the magic number—*the* guideline for productivity. In the original statement, national productivity figures of 2.4 per cent, 3.0 per cent, 3.5 per cent, and 2.6 per cent were given. Three different numbers were listed for manufacturing productivity, with variations according to time span and operating levels.

Moreover, the CEA gave all kinds of exceptions to its general rules. Wages would move up faster than the average if they were very low to start with; smaller increases would go to men who were exceptionally well paid. Likewise, special price consideration should be given to industries that were excessively profitable or unprofitable.

All the exceptions and qualifications gave the CEA

document an academic tone. At the same time, some of the variations went to the roots of the whole system. Special price restraints should be applied to an industry "in which the relation of productive capacity to full employment demand shows the desirability of an outflow of capital from the industry." Relatively small wage hikes were appropriate in an industry "which could not provide jobs for its entire labor force even in times of generally full employment."

These measures seemed to use the wage-price mechanism as an instrument for reshaping the economy. Decisions would be made not to achieve stability but to channel people and resources into different fields. Even without extending the concept in this manner, the wage-price guideline represented the first serious attempt to rationalize important economic functions.

The basic idea was ingenious and attractive. By having a single productivity standard, all classes of workers received equitable shares of progress. Moreover, a broad index tended to be the truest measure of productivity because it included the man-hours going into the creation of productive machines. For management, prices would fluctuate up or down according to an industry's ability to absorb the average increase. This ability would vary with the productivity of the industry. If the overall guideline was right, the price changes would balance out for overall stability.

The guidelines caused something of a stir when they were released in January, 1962. However, the only thought that really came through was that the government had come up with 3 per cent or some such number that had something to do with collective bargaining.

Walter Heller, CEA chairman in 1962, complained later that very few people had taken the trouble to read the guideline presentation. That was probably true. If people had read, they might have realized the new philosophy was something more formidable than it appeared. At the time, the guideline seemed to be simply a broad expression of objectives.

On February 23, at the Executive Club in Chicago, Arthur Goldberg corrected this impression. "In the past when government officials were called upon to assist in collective bargaining, their only aim was to achieve a settlement. Today, in the light of our government's commitments both at home and abroad, government must increasingly provide guidelines that are not only in the interest of the parties themselves but which also take into account the public interest. . . . No one wants government intervention, of course, but everyone expects the government to assert and define the national interest."

George Meany, who was in Miami at an AFL–CIO executive board meeting, said Goldberg was "infringing on the rights of a free people and a free society." Management spokesmen saw the nation taking another big step toward Bolshevism. If they didn't realize it before, steel men now knew they had gotten involved in something big and new.

On January 25, Roger Blough was called to the White House to a meeting with President Kennedy, Arthur Goldberg, and Dave McDonald, the Steelworkers chief. "Again I made it plain that U. S. Steel . . . would not engage in negotiations if price were involved in any way," said Roger Blough.* "I explained that I could not participate in negotiations if the bargaining had anything to do with price on three grounds: law, cost, and actual inability to make any commitment on prices. I further emphasized that U. S. Steel had not raised prices for almost four years—although our costs had shot skyward. . . ." Blough said the purpose of the meeting was to explore "the possibility of an early start to the 1962 negotiation."

Blough did not mention any discussion of terms but Pres-

* *Look,* January 29, 1963.

35

ident Kennedy is said to have offered some numbers in support of a wage hike of about 2.5 per cent. Some authorities insist the basic deal was wrapped up at this time and that subsequent talks were just playacting for the benefit of union members.

If that was true, the two sides did a good acting job. On February 6, Goldberg wired the 11 companies and the Steelworkers, calling for early negotiations and warning of the need to head off a steel inventory buildup. On February 8, the USWA wage-policy committee approved a set of demands calling for a wage increase and job security measures. Formal talks started February 14 on a cordial, hopeful note.

"The general attitude of the representatives in all these meetings appears to reflect a desire to get on with the work at hand and arrive at an early agreement," said R. Conrad Cooper. The meetings in question involved local union people and representatives of individual companies. At the time, they were partly therapeutic; local union officials sounded off and the companies responded but serious questions were reserved for top-level bargaining. On these serious questions, it looked as though the two sides were lining up for another slugfest. The union noted that the companies had made money "even when production fell below 50 per cent of capacity." With demand rising, said the Steelworkers, the industry was headed for "record profits."

One of the industry's crosses is that protective buying always lifts volume and profits in the middle of labor negotiations. Bargaining takes place in a boom atmosphere. After the settlement, users liquidate excess inventory and the steel business collapses.

In 1962, the companies noted that employment costs had risen 12 per cent over the previous 3 years while productivity was up only 6 per cent. Employment security would depend on "increased sale and production of American steel and American steel products," said management. At about this time, *U. S. News and World Report* came out with an interview of Roger Blough. In this, Blough dwelt on the steel cost squeeze, saying the recent trend couldn't continue indefinitely. He said any further wage hike would increase the pressure for action that much more. Blough thought this was pretty straight talk but coming in the middle of labor negotiations, it didn't register very strongly. People possibly were conditioned to complaints about steel profits while the industry was arguing its case for wage moderation.

On March 2, the labor talks were broken off. Dave McDonald said there was no point in continuing "fruitless discussions." The companies could see no "basis for settlement." The bargaining collapse came as a jolt to those who thought the whole deal was in the bag. However, there were no real blasts by the two sides. It didn't appear that anyone was very mad or excited.

Arthur Goldberg later insisted the stalemate was real and dangerous. He said it was "a major achievement of the Administration" that talks were kept on the track. "Second guessers overlook one fact—that there was a breakoff in negotiations. Those of us who are experienced in steel know that's an ominous sign. In the absence of quick movement, there would have been a full buildup of propaganda."

"If the companies had dug in at 4¢ or 5¢, which was an impossible settlement for the union, the situation could very well have drifted into a strike. And at the point the breakoff occurred, the companies were convinced that the union wasn't going to settle for less than 15¢ or 16¢, which the companies regarded as completely unreasonable." Some reports have it that Goldberg got the union to come down from 17¢ during the recess. He, himself, says nothing more than that the government got the two sides talking again.

At the time, an early resumption was regarded as a matter of routine certainty. "They'll wait a few days for the dust to settle," said a union bargainer. "Then, I imagine we'll get a call from the President to start talking again." President Kennedy's summons came March 8—6 days after the deadlock—and talks were started again on March 14.

That same day, a call for higher industry profits was issued by Leslie B. Worthington, U. S. Steel president. Industry needed to make more money if it was to meet world challenges, said Worthington. "We have channeled our gains for the most part into the areas of labor . . . and government. We have even spent future gains."

Reports from the bargaining table did not suggest any great movement during the recess. A steel company president said the industry was offering 8¢ an hour and the union was demanding 16¢. "If the government or anybody else thinks we're going to raise our offer in a hurry," he said, "they're in for a surprise."

A week later the gap was said to be still 8¢. "If you assume the market will not take a price increase, you have to assume this is our final offer," said a steel executive. He said he was so sure nothing would happen that he was going away for a 2-week vacation.

A day or two later the settlement was announced. The first story of the agreement came out of Washington—a little touch that reminded people of the Administration's assistance. In any case, there was a steel settlement. It had come 3 months before a strike deadline—without public recrimination or fuss. Because the contracts had not been officially reopened, there had never been a specific strike threat.

If all this was unprecedented for the steel industry, the contract terms were even more novel. They provided no wage increase; all benefits were in the area of job security. Company payments to Supplementary Unemployment Benefit (SUB) funds were increased 4½¢ an hour. Another 3¢ was provided for a savings and vacation plan.

It was agreed that SUB money could "spill over" into vacation programs. This proved fairly significant when the steel business boomed in 1964 and 1965. For Crucible Steel Co. of America, the various funds added up to an average vacation of 5 weeks a man in 1965.

Other major provisions involved a broadening of seniority rights. Men layed off in one department could bid for jobs in other departments or other plants. A labor pool was established for men in lower job classes. Subcontracting and other job security matters were referred to the Human Relations Committee for further study.

The contract had a nominal length of 2 years but the union could bargain and strike for practically anything after 1 year. It was an open-end agreement: terms would remain in effect until 90 days after the union served a reopening notice. The most important aspect, however, was the cost. The package was valued at 10¢ an hour for 1 year. This came to 2.5 per cent of steel labor costs. It compared with 3.5 per cent in the 1960 agreement and an average of 8 per cent a year from 1940 to 1959.

At the official signing on March 31, there was general rejoicing. Dave McDonald hailed new benefits as "a bold step toward relieving the anxiety of workers. . . ." Both sides hailed the contributions of the Human Relations Committee.

President Kennedy hailed the achievement of the bargainers in reaching an agreement so far in advance of the July 1 strike deadline. Speaking by phone to the union's wage-policy committee, the President went on to say the terms were "obviously non-inflationary and should provide a solid base for continued price stability." He indicated that the new doctrine of government intervention had been strengthened. "I am sure that the nation will agree with me that the most notable aspect of this settlement is that it demonstrates that the national interest can be protected. . . ."

Roger Blough said later that he was troubled by the President's remarks.* In their official statement at the time of the signing, the companies did offer a mild dissent. The 2.5 per cent agreement was a step in the right direction, they conceded, but it didn't go far enough. ". . . it exceeds by about 50 per cent the increase since 1940 of about 1.7 per cent per year in shipments of steel per manhour worked—which is a measurement that overstates the true gain of productivity." "While the terms of the settlement cannot be said to fall wholly within the limits of anticipated gains in productive efficiency," said R. Conrad Cooper, "they do represent real progress. . . ."

After the meeting, Marvin Miller of the Steelworkers was irked by the harping on the productivity gap. Cooper's remarks were out of keeping with the spirit of the negotiations, said Miller. But amid all the rejoicing, the small protest went unheard. Later accounts said this was the final bit of duplicity. The steel people had stood by silently while everyone talked about a settlement that would bring price stability. Steel executives, themselves, would not recall the words of dissent.

On this occasion as on many others in the preceding months, the steel men had failed to communicate their thinking. Although the trap had already closed, it might have lessened the later shock if the industry had been able to break through the cheerful chorus. Even those friendly to management were hailing the agreement. Morgan Guarantee Trust Co. said the moderate terms "provided the brightest word in recent weeks."

U. S. News and World Report said the settlement would have a "big effect on business sentiment." "The point is

* *Look,* January 29, 1963.

made that a major union in a basic industry for the first time since World War II has recognized the broad public interest in a new contract." The point also was that an Administration has asked labor to go easy. For years, businessmen had been complaining that the government was always after prices but would never say "Boo" to the unions about wages. Now the Kennedy Administration had said "No" on wages and made it stick.

That was the way it looked to the outside world, anyway. It's important to realize that the actual bargainers didn't see things in quite this light. "I think we were on the track of making an agreement by ourselves," recalls a company official. "The breakoff came after we had been wrestling with a lot of complicated programs. It seemed a good idea for everyone to take a breather." According to this official, there was no movement during the recess. He said the government's role in the bargaining had been overplayed. "They seemed anxious to take credit for every little thing that happened."

Another company man says top-level bargaining had quietly started in late 1961. He says the Administration was entirely aware of this when it made public its call for a start of negotiations February 6. Roger Blough makes no mention of earlier talks in his account of the January White House meeting. Company people were not alone in feeling the Administration had made a great show of managing something that had happened largely of its own accord.

Government pressure was the least important factor in the settlement, said Marvin Miller, a member of the union's bargaining team. More important, said Miller, was the memory of the 1959 strike. Also helpful, said he and others, was the work of the Human Relations Committee. The Committee had held 200 sessions since April of 1960. It had come up with joint recommendations on seniority, grievances, and arbitration. It had reached a partial understanding on job classification. "The most important thing had to do with the attitudes of people," said Miller. "We started with hostile mistrust on both sides. We ended with understanding."

William G. Caples, vice-president of industrial and public relations for Inland Steel Co., said the effort of the Human Relations Committee was "bargaining on a high level. . . . I think there is a much more mature relationship," he said. Labor Secretary Arthur Goldberg never claimed that the settlement terms were imposed on the parties. "It is a fact that a settlement was reached in the steel industry through free collective bargaining . . . ," he said.

But to the general public, all this was quibbling. The Administration had provided some degree of support and assistance in the negotiations. The companies had not rejected the government's help. The result had been a moderate settlement—a noninflationary settlement. It was a settlement that would not be followed by price increases.

On April 10, Edmund F. Martin, president of Bethlehem Steel Co., talked to reporters. Martin was quoted as saying: "There shouldn't be any price increase. We shouldn't do anything to increase our costs if we are to survive." Another version had Martin saying "competition in the United States and from foreign sources should result in price reductions." Bethlehem denied he said there should not be a hike "even after the new labor contract goes into effect. . . ." "Mr. Martin was, in fact, indefinite about the matter of prices," said the company's official statement.

That same day—April 10—a decision to increase steel prices was getting a final okay from U. S. Steel's executive committee. This 14-man body included Blough, Leslie Worthington, and finance chairman Robert C. Tyson. Most of the other members were from outside the steel industry. Three days previously, the price move had been approved by the operations policy committee, a 10-man body made up of U. S. Steel executives. The question of market acceptance was reportedly raised but there doesn't seem to have been any serious challenge in either committee.

Nearly 20 men, from a broad range of backgrounds, apparently had no doubts about what was certainly one of the most questionable business decisions in history. It's possible the dilution of responsibility made the executives less mindful of the risks. However, there is no question that Roger Blough is the boss of U. S. Steel. Finance chairman Tyson is a powerful force but Blough is the man, the final voice, the chief executive. In this particular situation, it might have been better if the committee system had been as cumbersome, slow and undecisive as it is supposed to be.

1962 · THE CONFRONTATION

At 5:15 P.M. on April 10, Blough entered the White
House and handed President Kennedy a copy of U. S.
Steel's price announcement. An across-the-board increase
of $6 a ton would take effect the next day. "Only by gener-
ating the funds necessary to keep . . . facilities fully
competitive can our company continue to provide its customers with a dependable source of steel and to provide its
employees with dependable jobs." Referring to prolonged
cost inflation, U. S. Steel called its move a "catch-up" increase.

The President glanced at the paper and called Arthur
Golberg. Goldberg asked why Blough had bothered to call
when the deed was already done—the announcement hit the
wire services at 7:00 P.M. Blough replied the call was a
courtesy. Goldberg didn't think so. He talked for a while.
A little before seven, Blough left.

The full meaning of the price increase apparently didn't
hit President Kennedy at once. From all accounts, he was
calm and quiet during the Blough visit. ". . . there was
no invective at that time, nor threats," recalled Blough.*

* *Look,* January 29, 1963.

But it quickly became apparent that the President, who never really convinced people he was an all-out liberal, was in trouble with labor and with the liberal wing of the party.

Dave McDonald was "surprised, troubled, and concerned." Arthur Goldberg was talking about resigning. It was only a matter of time before blasts would be coming from Senator Kefauver, Senator Gore, and the others.

It was not just the price matter that hung in the balance. The President's whole domestic program centered on helping business. For the first time in 30 years or more, an administration was trying to expand the economy not by spending more but by promoting growth in the private sector. Depreciation rules, a special concern of the steel industry, were being liberalized. The investment tax credit was being prepared. There was talk of an income tax cut. On top of all this, there had been the unprecedented business of talking moderation to labor.

These efforts put the President very much in the middle. His helping hand to business had aroused the suspicions of liberals. Business had said it didn't want any help that was tied to control of its commercial freedom. In this situation, Kennedy could hardly push forward with his program of tax reform. A year after the Bay of Pigs disaster, his grand scheme for the economy was falling apart. Resignations might destroy cabinet unity. The dashing vigor of the New Frontier would be exposed as an ineffectual fizzle.

However, the Administration decided to fight the price increase. After Blough left the White House Tuesday evening, Theodore Sorensen, CEA chairman Walter Heller, and other aides quickly gathered.* Phone calls went out to Attorney General Robert Kennedy; Secretary of Defense Robert S. McNamara; and Secretary of the Treasury C. Douglas Dillon, who was in Florida.

It was during these first milling moments that the Presi-

* *New York Times*, April 23, 1962.

dent cut loose with his remark about all businessmen or all steel men being SOBs. This comment shouldn't have been made by the President of the United States. There shouldn't have been a photographer around to hear it. Most of all, the remark should not have been printed by the *New York Times*. Businessmen and leaders in all fields use swear words every day. These are just casual expressions when heard. If printed, they would appear as hard, shocking judgments. For this reason—because there is distortion—and because it's understood they're off the record, profane ramblings seldom appear in print.

President Kennedy's cuss words were printed and his outburst was one of the minor incident's that tended to color the whole affair. Later reactions tended to be personal and emotional. However, the Kennedy team wasted little time in discussing. Within hours of the U. S. Steel announcement, Robert Kennedy had announced one price probe. "Because of past price behavior in the steel industry, the Department of Justice will take an immediate and close look at the current situation and any future developments."

Senator Kefauver was given the word by phone and soon had his statement ready. "I have ordered the staff of the subcommittee to begin an immediate inquiry into the matter." The Economic Advisers worked late into the night digging up numbers on steel prices and costs.

The next day, Wednesday, saw the steel companies getting a public pasting. Senator Hubert Humphrey said the increase was "an affront to the President and an irritant to labor." George Meany charged the mills with "wanton price gouging." Dave McDonald said his union had never negotiated an inflationary agreement.

The Administration was also putting out private lines. Edward Gudeman, Undersecretary of Commerce, gained a momentary place in history by calling Philip D. Block,

46

Jr., vice-chairman of Inland Steel Co.* Gudeman had attended Harvard School for boys with Block. He asked the steel man what he thought about the price increase. Block said that he was surprised. Gudeman indicated the Administration's opposition but he did not press for a decision.

In other moves during the crisis, government officials followed this soft line, asking for consideration but not threatening or pressuring. Inland Steel was spotted by the Administration as one of the more hopeful centers of resistance. Inland's officials tend to be less orthodox in their thinking than the average steel men. At least one top executive is an active Democrat. Inland's chairman, Joseph Leopold Block, spent 3 years as a dollar-a-year man with the War Production Board in World War II.

Heading a company founded by his grandfather, Joe Block had long been active in Community Chest, Chamber of Commerce, and Jewish charities. He stressed civic work in a code drawn up for Inland employees. Early in the game, he urged businessmen to shake off antigovernment leanings. "We hear some of our colleagues repeatedly assert that Government in a free society has no place whatsoever in economic affairs. But such a viewpoint is contrary to historic fact and totally unrealistic."

One other point made Inland a likely target—it was one of the more profitable companies in the industry. In 1961, its earnings rose $7 million and equaled 7.5 per cent of sales. The same year U. S. Steel's profit dropped more than $100 million and came to 5.7 per cent of sales. The whole industry earned something under 5.3 per cent on sales. The matter of profitability was probably not a key factor. Before and after the price action, Inland was as orthodox as anyone in its thinking that steel profits and prices were too low.

* *The New York Times,* April 23, 1962.

Various other lines went out. Secretary McNamara called Edward J. Hanley, president of Allegheny Ludlum Steel Corp. President Kennedy called Edgar F. Kaiser, head of Kaiser Steel Corp. Walter Heller is said to have checked Armco Steel. In addition to the Gudeman call, Inland Steel officials were contacted by Arthur Goldberg and Henry Fowler.*

However, it looked as though the tide was running against the Administration. Shortly after noon on Wednesday, Bethlehem Steel announced it was following U. S. Steel on the increases. Republic, Youngstown, Jones & Laughlin, and Wheeling Steel Corp. joined the move. At about 3:30 P.M. on Wednesday, President Kennedy delivered a prepared statement at his televised press conference. "The simultaneous and identical action of United States Steel and other leading steel companies increasing prices by some six dollars a ton constitutes a wholly unjustifiable and irresponsible defiance of the public interest."

The President recited the perils facing the nation and the sacrifices being made. ". . . the American people will find it hard as I do to accept a situation in which a tiny handful of steel executives, whose pursuit of private power and profit exceeds their sense of public responsibility, can show such utter contempt for the interest of one hundred and eighty-five million Americans." The government's statistics were trotted out. Steel productivity was rising, the increase would add $1 billion to defense costs, general inflation would result, the companies had record profits in the first quarter, the settlement had been modest.

The President closed with these stinging words: "Some time ago I asked each American to consider what he could do for his country and I asked the steel companies. In the last 24 hours, we had their answer." It was a thrilling oration that Roger Blough was waiting in the wings to follow.

* *New York Times,* April 23, 1962.

Rarely in modern times had a leader made such a magnificent appeal for the support of the people.

Yet, it was excessive. It would take time for the applause to subside but there would be a gradual reaction as people realized Roger Blough was not, after all, a Julius Caesar plotting to take over the republic. In the press questioning that followed, President Kennedy's answers were direct and effective. There had been no specific promise on prices "but I did clearly emphasize on every occasion that my only interest was in trying to secure an agreement which would not provide an increase in prices. . . . Our whole purpose in attempting to persuade the union was for the purpose of maintaining price stability. . . . That thread ran through every discussion I had or Secretary Goldberg."

There was no promise but "at no time did anyone suggest that if such an agreement was gained it would still be necessary to put up prices." President Kennedy made no threat of formal price controls. In this extreme moment, he made no final statement on withdrawing depreciation reforms. The President also avoided any attempt to make his case better than it was. He conceded there had been no specific price commitment. He admitted the price action was entirely legal; freedom in wage and price matters "did and should exist."

The President's words were convincing because he did make concessions and didn't try to argue points that couldn't be argued. This approach focused attention on the strong points of the Administration's case. It made the presentation straightforward and clear.

At 6 P.M. on Wednesday, the Attorney General ordered the FBI to check out the statement of Edmund Martin of Bethlehem. FBI men rousted out a wire service reporter at 3 A.M. the next morning. They were told the quote was correct. Like the SOB remark, this early morning visit was a trivial incident that was to stick in the minds of people.

Congressman William E. Miller charged Gestapo tactics. The Administration tried to shrug the charge off, saying the FBI didn't like to waste time. President Kennedy later pointed out that reporters have been known to disturb people in their homes at night. Nevertheless, the menacing picture of troupers in the night did remain.

Chairman Paul Rand Dixon of the Federal Trade Commission said he was checking for possible violation of an earlier consent decree. Archibald Cox, the Solicitor General, advised the President that present antitrust laws were inadequate. Cox began drafting new legislation.

In Washington, Congressman Emanuel Celler announced that subcommittee hearings, scheduled for May 2, might consider antitrust amendments. Senator Gore called for legislation that could require a "cooling-off" period before price increases took effect. Senator Kefauver promised an investigation. House Speaker John McCormack called the price increase "shocking."

In New York, Roger Blough prepared for his ordeal—a press conference the next day. "I had decided on a temperate answer," said Blough, "although it would have relieved a lot of tension and frustration if I had yielded to natural impulses as others in the industry did later." * Congressman William Scranton of Pennsylvania was preparing this comforting wire for Blough: "The increase at this time is wrong—wrong for Pennsylvania, wrong for America, wrong for the free world" (sent on Thursday).

On Thursday, the Administration seemed to be gaining public support. The *New York Herald Tribune* said the increases were "regrettable to put it mildly." The *New York Times* spoke of "irresponsible defiance. . . ." Walter Lippmann thought the companies had made a "rude" decision. The *St. Louis Post-Dispatch* gave this analysis. "It looks very much as if the steel masters used the President

* *Look,* January 29, 1963.

50

and his Secretary of Labor for the purpose of beating down wage demands prior to a price decision they had in mind all along."

But if the Administration was winning the hearts of the nation, it was losing a very vital minority. On Thursday, National Steel Corp. and Pittsburgh Steel Co. joined in the price increases. There was no letup in the pressure for a rollback. FBI agents were hitting the mills with subpoenas for price data. Administration officials were continuing informal contacts with the companies, including U. S. Steel.

Thursday afternoon, Blough went on TV with his answer to the President. He gave the general economics of the move. "Hourly employment costs have increased since 1958 by a total of 12 per cent. . . . Our own profit of 5.7 per cent on sales in 1961 was the lowest since 1952 . . . (the increase would) add almost negligibly to the cost of steel which goes into the familiar, everyday products that we use." The cost in an auto would be about $10 and in a toaster 3¢, he said. On the matter of profits, Blough did not note that U. S. Steel's shipments in 1961 were the worst since 1946. He cited President Kennedy's statement to the effect that no assurances on price had been asked or given. On the business of concealing price intentions, he quoted from the February 16 interview in *U. S. News & World Report*. " 'Even now there should be a remedy' " he had said. " 'If any additional cost occurs, the necessity for the remedy becomes even greater.' " Like other pronouncements, this statement was a double-edged bit of evidence.

Where Blough had his greatest difficulty was in trying to explain the competitive reasoning of U. S. Steel. He was asked: How can you meet foreign and other competition by raising prices? Blough said he had already answered the question but added: "If you do not provide the new plant and equipment that is necessary to keep up with foreign competition, you are going to fall behind in the race that

51

much further than you have." Another version of this thought went like this: "I said you become noncompetitive, your costs are higher, if you have insufficient prices to provide the machinery and equipment that are necessary to remain competitive." Blough's exposition seemed deficient on two counts: clarity and candor. He insisted on running separate thoughts together—on equating competition with price increases and cost reduction.

Official steel statements tend to do this. Steel men today will speak of the need for competitive freedom as though someone were forbidding them to cut prices. They do face competition and they may need to raise prices but the two considerations are not identical. This obscurity of expression possibly stems from the preoccupation of the steel men with their troubles. They are always arguing against the demands of labor, the evils of big government, and the unfairness of import competition.

One of Roger Blough's big jobs has been as public advocate of steel objectives and a defender against the enemies of steel. This constant concern with steel's side of the story has not been calculated to develop broad objectivity. "The steel people have been talking about depreciation so long they almost believe it themselves," said the head of one diversified company. One top union official insists that through long obfuscation, steel management has lost the power of direct communication. "It's not that they don't want to simplify things. It's just that they don't know how to anymore."

It should be pointed out that steel men have had a lot to defend against over the years. Nevertheless, repeated reciting of the party line is not the best schooling for grasping diverse viewpoints. At any rate, Roger Blough could not see, or he would not admit, the flaws in his position. He couldn't say: "Of course, the price increase will make us less competitive but it means we'll live to fight another day." He couldn't say: "Maybe I should have been more definite but if you're not careful these days, they'll throw you into jail for collusion."

As it was, Blough refused to concede a point. The lack of concession made his argument fuzzy. It meant his words failed to carry a ring of candor. And it was candor the steel people needed to demonstrate. The issue was not just whether an increase was needed or not. The big question was whether a deliberate deception had been practiced. If Roger Blough failed to resolve this question, he did dispel the picture of arrogance that President Kennedy had left.

Blough's manner, his appearance and his delivery all gave the impression of simplicity and humility. A tall, solidly built man, Blough's face is strong but not belligerent. There are lines of sorrow. He looked like what he was: a man of fortitude and forebearance who was taking a cruel beating. The initial reaction within the industry was that Blough had done a weak job of stating the case. He certainly didn't turn the tide against President Kennedy. Yet the contrast between the President's anger and Blough's mildness did raise doubts. There would be a delayed reaction of sympathy toward the steel executive.

Meanwhile, the break had come although no one knew it. Inland Steel had decided not to increase prices. Unfortunately, Joe Block, Inland's chairman, was in Japan. He was contacted by phone and concurred in a decision by the Inland board. However, the public announcement was not to be made until the next day—Friday. The delay provided time for actions and words that would have lasting implications. At 5 P.M. on Thursday, Commerce Secretary Hodges renewed the public campaign in a press conference.

"Any firm or industry is free to set prices as it sees fit. It is free to make mistakes and I believe the steel industry's mistake is a basic one. Its action is a disservice to the country and the business community. . . ." The price increase was ordered "by a handful of men who said, in effect, that U.S. Steel comes first and the United States of America second."

Privately, Administration officials were continuing to needle U. S. Steel through direct and indirect channels. At 7 P.M., Robert Kennedy announced the Justice Department had authorized a grand jury investigation in New York. This was one of the moves that was to make the confrontation a lingering problem.

On Friday at 11:45 A.M., the Defense Department announced that "where possible, procurement for steel will be shifted to those companies which have not increased prices. I consider in my judgment the price increase was an unjustified development," said Robert McNamara. He explained that the "fanning out of the price increase" would boost defense cost by $1 billion or $3\frac{1}{2}$ per cent.

Roger Blough had pointed out that no more than $3\frac{1}{2}$ million tons of steel were going into defense projects. He said the cost would be "something in the nature of $20 million." McNamara insisted the boost would jeopardize both the defense effort and the balance of payments position.

By this time, Inland Steel's position had been made known. The *Chicago Daily News* published an interview with Joe Block in Japan. "We do not feel that an advance in steel prices at this time would be in the national interest," said Mr. Block. At 10 A.M., the official Inland announcement was released. Word reached the White House at noon, while the President was saying goodbye to the Shah of Iran. Also at this time came the word that Kaiser was not planning to increase prices. Armco Steel Corp. had said nothing but had not moved either.

Among White House strategists, there had been much fussing about the number of holdouts it would take to block the increase. Someone had come up with the figure 16 per cent. To steel people, it was inconceivable that the increase could stick unless every one of the major mills supported it. With demand collapsing and with Inland located in the heart of the big sheet markets, it was simply a question of time before others fell back.

Price probers can't seem to grasp the fact that identical steel prices are based on identical standard products. The probers stress the point that no one is charging a lower price than the rest of the industry. Steel men put it the other way, saying no one is able to charge a higher price.

Nevertheless, there was suspense after the Inland announcement as everyone waited for the next move. Administration officials were closeted in a hotel with U. S. Steel executives on Friday afternoon. Like so much of what had been done by them in the past 12 months, this informal heckling seemed superfluous. The price increase was already doomed but the Administration had to involve itself in the final victory.

The official surrender came at 3 P.M. on Friday the 13th when Bethlehem Steel rescinded its increases. Known within the industry as a company with commercial and technical savvy, Bethlehem did not cover itself with glory in the price crisis. One of its top executives was caught with his mouth open just before the increase. It had been the first company to follow in the boost. And now it was the first to retract.

There was speculation that because of its shipbuilding operations, Bethlehem was particularly vulnerable to defense blacklisting. It's possible the company felt there might be special embarrassment arising from Martin's comments. More than likely, it was a simple case of not wanting to lose orders to Inland and Kaiser. In any case, its rollback officially killed the increase. "Although we still hold the opinion that a steel price increase is needed," said Arthur B. Homer, Bethlehem chairman, "we must remain competitive. For the ultimate good and future welfare of our economy, we must have lower costs to permit lower prices for successful world competition and improved volume of business and employment."

Shortly after 5 P.M. U. S. Steel threw in the sponge. The increase in prices was being rescinded, said president Leslie Worthington, "in the light of competitive developments today and all other current circumstances including the removal of a serious obstacle to proper relations between government and business." Republic, Jones & Laughlin, and the others quickly followed. President Kennedy said the people of the United States were "most gratified." Work on new wage-price legislation was suspended. As a parting shot, however, U. S. Steel and Bethlehem were shut out of a $5 million defense order. The job went to Lukens Steel Co.

In Pittsburgh, black clouds appeared over the U. S. Steel building as employees scurried for their 5:30 buses.

1962 · THE BACKWASH

The battle had ended but the shock wave continued. For the nation's creative writers and others it was a rare occasion for rich prose. At the time the labor settlement was being hailed, wrote Arthur Krock in the Saturday *Times,* "the leading company was already in the process of shattering the expectation implicit in his praise." On Sunday a *Times* editorial said: "The forces of our democracy scored a dramatic triumph last week." On Monday, the papers told that the President's triumph was being hailed in Brazil. The victory was also hailed by Robert Frost. Across the aisle in Congress, Senator Everett Dirkson called for "a less punitive spirit in government." *Iron Age* magazine referred to the display of "naked power." Steel men were outraged by the Administration's whimsical, intemperate behavior, *Iron Age* said.

On Monday, Senator Humphrey proposed a commission to probe the steel industry. Senator Gore asked for a law that would break up big corporations. "The plain fact of the matter," he said, "is that United States Steel sets the price pattern for the whole steel industry." He said U. S.

Steel was run by "money market manipulators." Also on Monday, Senator Kefauver released a list of 12 steel companies whose cost figures were being subpoenaed by his antitrust subcommittee.

In a later article, Arthur Krock really tied himself in knots: "Never have so many owed to so few words an illustration of the incapacity of some big business managers to comprehend their public obligation as when Roger M. Blough, chairman of United States Steel Corporation, replied to a news conference question last Thursday. Asked if he was surprised, Blough replied 'I think the answer to that should be that I was.' " For Krock this was "an intolerable strain on human credulity or an admission of incurable shortsightedness."

Meanwhile, the principals were trying to bury the whole mess. On Monday, Blough visited with President Kennedy for 45 minutes. At his press conference April 18, the President spoke conciliatory words. ". . . let me make it clear that this Administration harbors no ill will. Our goals of economic growth and price stability are dependent upon the success of both . . . business and labor." He said he was not "unmindful of the steel industry's needs for profits, modernization, and investment capital."

The President noted that he was preparing a provision whereby 8 per cent of a capital investment could be taken as a tax credit. He said the Treasury Department was working to reform depreciation guidelines. He said the government's whole policy was directed at promoting economic growth. Finally, he denied that the Administration was seeking control of wages or prices. "This is a free economy. These matters are reached by the process and completion of collective bargaining." The President did not say the grand jury price probe was being called off. This sore was left to fester.

On April 19, the Republicans finally got untracked and

took a stand. They cited these government steps: (1) The FTC suggestion of a collusion probe. (2) The Justice Department probe. (3) The Treasury Department review of depreciation. (4) Menacing moves by the Internal Revenue Service toward U. S. Steel's incentive benefit plan. (5) The senate antitrust committee probe. (6) The Justice Department Grand Jury investigation. (7) The Defense Department shift of business. (8) The FBI invasion of reporters' homes. "Taken collectively," said the Republicans, "these actions amounted to a display of naked political power never seen before in this nation. We condone nothing in the actions of the steel companies except their right to make an economic judgment without massive retaliation by the Federal government. Should a President . . . use the enormous powers of the Federal government to blackjack any segment of our free society?"

John M. Bailey, chairman of the Democratic National Committee, had this reply: "The question is, were they for or against the price increase? If they were against it, how could they have protected the public? If they were for it, why not tell that to the people?"

And that, of course, was the hell of it for steel people. The big test of free enterprise had come in a manner that did not give a clear choice. For many conservatives, even, it was not a question of right against wrong. The President was wrong, but it was difficult to defend the industry in righteous tones.

This difficulty was increased April 26 when U. S. Steel and Bethlehem were indicted for fixing prices of steel forgings. Midvale-Heppenstall Co., Erie Forge & Steel Corp., and the Open Die Forging Institute, Inc., were also named in the indictment. Homer Lackey, who had been manager of forgings at U. S. Steel, was indicted along with Erb Gurney and Robert S. Barnes, who headed forgings and casting sales at Bethlehem.

There was apparently no connection between this case and the April 10 price hike. The grand jury in the forgings case had begun hearing testimony in December, 1961. Its indictment said the companies had rigged bids on Navy ordnance and electrical forgings. It was charged that the companies reported to their Institute all requests for quotations over $500. Price talks then followed by phone or at the association, U. S. Steel allegedly worked through Bethlehem.

The heavy forgings industry was in a depressed state at this time. Jack Roche, president of Heppenstall Co., had noted in 1961 that his company was selling medium forgings at prices lower than 5 years earlier. Erie Forge, which Homer Lackey had headed since September 1, 1960, was close to going out of business. U. S. Steel had only 4 per cent of the heavy forging business and this product line accounted for less than 1 per cent of its dollar sales. As these figures indicate, forgings are not really part of the basic steel industry. Although the two biggest mills happen to be in the business, forge shops are not considered steel companies.

So it was not, in a sense, steel prices that were involved. And it was not a matter of gouging customers but of trying to keep body and soul together. The forging business was in a depressed state. U. S. Steel seems to have been a very junior partner from the standpoint of both volume and initiative. But there was not room for all these quibbles in headlines. There was only room for the most damaging simplification: "U. S. Steel Indicted for Fixing Prices."

At more or less the same time they were invoking the doctrine of free competitive enterprise, the steel people had allegedly been rigging prices. On April 29, a *Times* article by Adolph Berle, Jr., indicated that no one should have been surprised. ". . . the power of big industry to 'administer' a price has been known to students for years."

The term "administer," if it was not being used sarcastically, meant that a concentrated industry could put through increases in an arbitrary manner without actual collusion. The forgings case suggested there were at least isolated bugs in this theory.

Another rap against the administered price theory came from Edward Hanley, president of Allegheny Ludlum. "Some of the steel companies misjudged their markets in some respects," said Hanley. He said Allegheny Ludlum "had no intention of increasing prices on many of our product lines. The President and his advisers did not give old-fashioned economics a real chance to work. I feel certain, if they had, many of the announced price increases would have been rescinded by now without the help of a Presidential whiplashing. . . ."

Allegheny Ludlum's two main products were stainless steel and electrical steel. Both were getting hit by price cuts. In the 5 years starting with 1958, Allegheny's stainless prices dropped 25 per cent. Its electrical steels were upgraded four or five times. In viewing his own company's steel market, Hanley could say very truthfully and sincerely that price competition was too fierce to even think of increases.

On a tonnage basis, however, stainless is only 1 per cent of the steel market. Electrical sheet is another small fraction. There were other pockets of weakness in the steel picture—linepipe, merchant wire, and rebars were usually problem products. In nearly all of these areas, the big mills faced competition from importers, from small steel companies, or from distributors who operated on a discount basis.

But there was no serious price cutting in markets for the tonnage carbon steel products—plates, structurals, bars, and sheets. As the mills themselves had said in 1961, prices of most important products were firm. Throughout the 5-

year slump of heavy industry, tonnage producers had been able to resist the attempts of purchasing agents to get major concessions. "Steel is the only material we've never been able to package," said the buyer for a large electrical company. And throughout the postwar period, every general steel increase had received general support. It is true the 1962 effort came when users were liquidating inventory and the steel market was falling apart. But the 1958 hike had been rammed through in a weak market.

In short, there is no reason to believe, as some commentators have argued, that commercial forces by themselves would have rolled back all the increases or most of them. Both before and after the crisis, Inland Steel was among those most vehement in saying increases were warranted on a purely commercial basis. On November 5, vice-chairman Philip Block described the industry as "bedeviled by foreign competition and a profit squeeze. And at the appropriate time," he said, "steel prices must be increased." None of the millions of words written gave a good answer to the $64 question: Why did U. S. Steel increase prices April 10?

It goes without saying that the top executives were convinced of the financial need. It is worth noting that finance people have a big voice in U. S. Steel affairs. Corporate headquarters are in downtown New York, in the heart of the financial community. The banking interests are represented on the top committee. Finance chairman Robert Tyson reports directly to the board; he does not go through the chief executive.

From a strictly financial viewpoint, the matter was straightforward. U. S. Steel had been spending $200 million a year on a new plant. That wasn't enough. ". . . you need to replace one twenty-fifth of your plant each year," said Robert Tyson. "For U. S. Steel, that would mean spending more than $400 million a year, not to expand, but just to stay even." The proposed 7 per cent tax credit would "not be enough to stimulate spending or solve basic problems." Depreciation changes still left companies open to "recrimination in after-the-fact redetermination by the government." (This threat has been tentatively eased.)

Price cuts wouldn't solve U. S. Steel's problem of contracting volume. "If customers don't buy more steel, there isn't too much you can do about it. . . . I doubt that you would go out and buy two new cars instead of one if steel prices were cut. . . ." Price levels couldn't be set on the expectation of higher sales. "Over the long pull, American steel mills have operated at about a 75 per cent average of capacity. If you operate at 90 per cent over a stretch, you've then got to figure on a stretch at 60 per cent of capacity. Basically, you must be able to make adequate profits at the average."

What would be the worst thing in the world? "The worst thing that could happen is to continue to go down this profit-squeeze road. Profits provide the money that provides the tools that provide the jobs." U. S. Steel didn't have any plans for outside financing. "Regardless of how you finance spending, the money must eventually be earned by the company."

Some of these points could be contested. It might be true that adequate profits should be made in an average year. But 1961 hadn't been average; it had been awful for U. S. Steel—the worst on shipments since 1946. The fatalistic attitude toward sales and prices was realistic in the short term, but over the years, price increases had cost the steel industry business. But there was no question U. S. Steel firmly and sincerely believed a price hike was needed in 1962. The big question involved the manner of the increase—the timing and the setting.

"As any merchant knows," said Roger Blough, "it is

the height of commercial folly to announce in advance a rise in prices if you do have such a plan." * The best time to boost a price, he said, was when no one expected it. This seems to be another case of running opposing thoughts together. It is possibly good strategy to cut prices without advance warning. This gives the cutter a chance to grab orders before the competition can collect its wits. But for a price increase, it's considered prudent to sound out the market. In some cases, this is a euphemism for getting a reaction from competitors. And in some cases outside steel, this is done in the most direct possible manner.

Another Blough argument was that the business climate was better in April than in October. It's questionable whether the general economy was very much better. With users liquidating inventory, the steel business certainly didn't seem so good. By a process of elimination, you almost have to say the steel price increase was a calculated challenge to the Administration. Steel people had made statements against federal intervention. When the price question came up in 1961, Roger Blough blasted the idea of government guidance.

None of these words made much impression. They did nothing to slow the headlong involvement of the Administration with wages and prices. And the steel-labor settlement had served to strengthen and encourage the whole guideline doctrine. Nothing the industry could say would check the trend. Some powerful action was needed. So U. S. Steel came up with its shocking price action. It goes without saying that the calculated defiance involved gross miscalculation. Roger Blough wasn't surprised that President Kennedy got mad. But Blough and others certainly didn't foresee the scope and the intensity of the reaction.

This seems an astounding mistake now. Everyone's think-

* *Look*, January 29, 1963.

ing now is conditioned by the manner in which Kennedy did react. With that precedent, it's unthinkable that U. S. Steel would increase prices the way it did in 1962. But it's important to remember the Administration's action was unprecedented. Steel mills had been increasing prices regularly for years. There had been problems but no one had ever declared war on a price increase before. And the industry, after all, did have every legal right to raise prices.

The price increase was a miscalculation but it was not as bad as it seemed afterward. There shouldn't have been as strong a kickback. The Administration was wrong in the ferocity of its chastisement. At an April 24 press conference, Blough was apparently still reeling from the effects of the blowup. "We believe," he said, "that an important public relations gain was made as a by-product of the recent controversy. . . . We have seen clear evidence in Washington that our actions have served as a catalyst in generating more widespread understanding that we cannot have a strong American industry without adequate profit."

The Administration did seem anxious to make amends and it was pushing ahead with the tax reforms planned earlier. But to say the industry had improved its public relations must certainly have made the steel image-builders cringe. Other mill executives had no illusions. E. B. Germany, head of Lone Star Steel Co., had this comment: "The victory of government over steel will be reflected in all industries for years to come. No company or industry may now raise prices without harboring the fear, and justifiably so, that the government may decide to display the crushing weapons so recently displayed."

Arthur Goldberg likewise recognized the government's labor intervention would have permanent effects. "I think it is both timely and just to say that the 1962 steel settlement will become firmly fixed as a development of great magnitude in our economic life."

It was clear the wage-price clash was too big and basic to be buried. The hostility created could not be talked away. The precedent established was too powerful to be ignored. The issue had been joined too openly for the Administration to retreat too far. On May 1, the President's Advisory Committee on Labor Management Policy recommended new federal powers for dealing with strike situations. The Committee said Taft-Hartley boards should be empowered to recommend terms. It said the President should be able to initiate a cooling-off period without an injunction.

A dissenting opinion came from Henry Ford, II, chairman of Ford Motor Co., and a member of the committee along with Joe Block of Inland Steel. "It is difficult to understand how the advocacy of a more dominant government roll in collective bargaining process can make for more freedom in this process," Ford said. The same day, Clarence B. Randall said the public attitude toward labor and management was one of a "plague on both your houses." Formerly chairman of Inland Steel, Randall had served on various government missions and had come to be regarded as a statesman. He suggested the industry might find itself "controlled like a public utility in the public interest." Dr. Arthur F. Burns, who had been head of the CEA under President Eisenhower, said big labor disputes had their origin "in the monopoly power of private groups."

On May 3, Arthur Krock chided the Chamber of Commerce for the cool reaction of its members to a Kennedy speech. Kennedy was, said Krock, "the first Democratic president since Woodrow Wilson . . . to require the same consideration of the public interest from organized labor that he required from management." Businessmen responded by sitting on their hands and closing their minds.

On May 4, Governor Nelson Rockefeller called for "cooperative effort." On May 7, Senator Barry Goldwater charged the President with depressing "the entire economic climate." Businessmen were left with "the kind of fear and uncertainty that deadens economic progress." On May 7, Blough called for "better understanding of the economic problems and profit needs of the entire business community." Two days later, the President said the Administration "cannot settle labor matters in disputes across the country."

On May 18, the President had a "useful and friendly" discussion with H. Ladd Plumley, head of the Chamber of Commerce. Plumley praised the Administration's tax reforms. The price intervention was blasted on May 18 by Richard Nixon and on May 24 by Allison R. Maxwell, Jr., president of Pittsburgh Steel Co. Nixon spoke of control by "executive whim." Maxwell parodied the President's original blast, describing "a tiny handful of government officials, in the pursuit of monopoly power over business. . . ." Henry Ford, II, issued another warning on the trend toward government intervention. U. S. Steel, on May 27, released a manifesto on the economic justification for the increase.

On May 28 the stock market crashed. The loss of $20.8 billion was double that of any 1929 day. If businessmen were not glad about this, they certainly had the satisfaction of knowing where the blame lay. "There is plenty of evidence around that business confidence in government is at a fairly low ebb," said Roger Blough on June 4. "The stock market reacted to this and research proves it to be true."

Mr. Blough was not vindictive. The man who engineered a defiant challenge of the President and the man who suffered most from this, Blough never displayed personal bitterness during or after the crisis. He called for better relations with government and said he was not sure business was "really doing its share. Confidence needs support on both sides. Business could do much more to inspire confidence."

Blough went on to call for depreciation reforms far more

sweeping than those being prepared by the President. There is no doubt he was sincere in the call. U. S. Steel had been calling for years for a faster write-off of facilities. There was no doubt either that the price rollback had a tangible and psychological impact. "We've been through the ringer since 1958," said one steel controller. "We don't have any fat left."

That was true. Wholesale personnel cuts had left the steel companies with little room for belt tightening. The price rollback had to come from capital programs. Suppliers of steel-mill equipment said there was an immediate reaction to the rollback. "Things that were supposed to be very active a few months ago are not active now," said Clark H. Johnson, vice-president, sales, United Engineering and Foundry Co. "People are frightened, I guess," said Ward Powell, vice-president, Mesta Machine Co. "We have orders in progress and people have called to see what could be done to stop them. That's very unusual in our business."

For some steel projects, it was not only unusual but impossible. Whether they liked the President or were disturbed by the price mess, some companies were fully committed to programs. Armco Steel said it was going ahead with plans to spend $100 million during the next year. Pittsburgh Steel was following through on its $44 million project. Jones & Laughlin still planned to spend $265 million for the next 3 years.

It did seem in this period that business people were not only determined to make the worst of things but were reacting in a perverse manner to offers of help. On both the investment credit and the depreciation change, the business attitude was one of either outright opposition or grudging support. The reforms weren't enough, said executives. The budget should be balanced first; the changes wouldn't really help. "What do they think this is," snorted a Wall Street analyst, "a Republican administration?"

An equipment executive believed there was simply an

68

emotional unwillingness to admit President Kennedy could do anything good. The President himself had some shrewd observations of the question of popularity. "I read that the problem really is that business confidence may be somewhat shaken by the action of certain public figures. Now business had a high confidence in the previous Administration yet there was a recession in 1958 and a recession in 1960. And in 1956, there was a sharp drop in the stock market before a very good year in 1957."

And it was a fact that business was getting an unprecedented lift from the government it hated. The new guidelines reduced the suggested life of steel equipment from an average of 25 years to 18 years. Actual depreciation had been running at about 23 years at the time. This meant a cut of something like 20 per cent in the depreciation term. For the whole industry this amounted to $114 million a year. For Jones & Laughlin, which was one of the few steel companies to show real enthusiasm for the change, depreciation increased $10 million a year. Although only half of this was a net gain, it did look as though nearly half the money lost in the price hassle would be recovered in this one tax reform.

Jones & Laughlin estimated the price hike would have boosted its earnings $12 million a year. The depreciation change added roughly $5 million to J. & L.'s cash flow. The investment tax credit for steel companies amounted to nearly $90 million in 1965. And all of this was a net addition to income under the amended provisions of the law.

Certainly, the direct tax benefits went a long way toward offsetting the price loss. How much indirect stimulus was provided can't be measured, but all evidence suggests the reforms helped promote a general boom. In 1963, steel output was to go over 100 million tons for the first time in 5 years. These results might have healed steel scars if someone could have stopped the actions set in motion April 10. It didn't work that way.

On June 25, word came that phone records and expense accounts of U. S. Steel, Bethlehem, and eight other steel companies had been subpoenaed by the Justice Department. The move was in connection with the grand jury probe started April 12. Despite recent sweet talk, the Administration could not or would not call off all its dogs.

On June 29, Allegheny Ludlum cut stainless sheet and plate prices 5 per cent. This was partly offset by a reduction in jobber discounts from 10 per cent to 5 per cent. In effect, this was raising the price to the jobber, who sold most of the sheet and plate. The problem of discounts was an unending one for stainless-steel people. If they made too big an allowance, the warehouse would give away part of its commission to get business. If they attempted to reduce the allowance, some producer would start making concessions to get business. Eventually, everyone would drop the base price and enlarge the discount again.

On July 1, nothing happened to steel prices when labor cost went up under the new contract. There was no increase. There was not even speculation about an increase. "If we even mentioned the word, price," said one steel man, "they'd stand us up against a wall and shoot us."

On July 25, another of the loose ends in the early controversy cropped up when Senator Kefauver demanded that Bethlehem Steel provide cost data for his antitrust subcommittee. U. S. Steel and some of the others had indicated they would provide the figures. Bethlehem refused on the grounds that the disclosure would give aid and comfort to foreign producers and other competition. Republic, National Steel, and Armco aligned themselves with Bethlehem in this position.

There were indications the Administration would have preferred that Senator Kefauver let well enough alone. On August 2, Arthur Goldberg again denied the government was adopting a policy of wholesale intervention. "We should encourage the parties to use their own procedures," he said. He saw a need to reduce the 5.3 per cent unemployment rate but he indicated that a shorter workweek would be inflationary. Also in August, the 7 per cent tax credit was approved by Congress.

The steel companies had taken one bad beating. Republic had cut its dividend. Avery Adams predicted a general profit slide. Joe Block of Inland was now saying higher prices were needed. Just as a matter of taste, it didn't seem the time for another public grilling. Nevertheless, Senator Kefauver was determined to have his day. He called the companies to appear August 31. They refused, saying this would prejudice their case. On September 1, a contempt citation was referred to the Senate Judiciary Committee. On September 12, the companies argued their case before the committee, and on September 25 they were cleared of contempt charges.

The matter was probably decided strictly along political lines. The committee was controlled by Republicans and conservative Democrats. The latter included: Senator James Eastland, Mississippi, chairman; Senator Samuel Ervin, Jr., North Carolina; Senator John McClellan, Arkansas; and Senator Olin Johnston, South Carolina.*

"I don't blame them for not submitting the data," said Senator Eastland after the hearing. "If the companies submitted the data on a confidential basis," said Senator Hugh Scott, "it would appear in the columns of somebody's favorite columnist. There are no secrets in Washington." "The national security was involved," said Senator McClellan.

So the steel people had at least a consolation victory. In a September 25 letter to the *Times,* Henry Steele Commager contrasted this action with extended contempt proceedings against eight Communists who refused to answer congressional questions. "Meanwhile," wrote Commager, "the heads of the great steel corporations who openly de-

* *The New York Times,* Sept. 26, 1962.

fied a subcommittee of the U. S. Senate and who refused to put in an appearance are not even cited for contempt." He concluded this was discriminatory justice.

This dig from the world of scholarship confused justice with some sort of rigid, legalistic symmetry. The steel people were not suspected of conspiring to overthrow the nation. Their crime in the Kefauver hearing was a matter of fairness rather than law; the Senator was seeking to determine if steel costs warranted a price hike. Because he had only recently quizzed the steel people on costs and because the Justice Department was already digging into the criminal question, it could be argued that the senate probe constituted double or triple jeopardy. And again, the steel industry had already been subjected to a public and financial mauling.

While this bit was being played out, the steel union was already talking it up for the next bargaining round. The union's convention, which is normally held in Atlantic City, moved to Miami Beach that year. In steamy mid-September weather, delegates discussed the bleak outlook for the steel industry. "In basic steel," said Dave McDonald, "there has been a diminishing of employment of almost 100,000."

Steelworker membership had dropped from over 1.2 million to 900,000. The labor content of steel had dropped from 17.1 hours per ton in 1958 to 13.9 hours in 1962. Just to stay even, said the union, steel output would have to rise to 115 million tons in 1962 and to 125 million tons by 1965. These were described as levels "not likely to be achieved in a peacetime economy." It did, indeed, appear that steel was a permanently depressed industry. Output had been below 100 million tons since 1957. Forecasters were saying it might be 1970 or 1975 before normal demand equaled the peaks of 1955 and 1956.

1962 · PICKING UP THE PIECES

The union's answer to all this was a reduction in working time. The Steelworkers realized it was futile to talk about a shorter work week; the cost would have been prohibitive and the Administration was against it. Accordingly, it was decided to reduce hours by increasing vacations. Dave McDonald had picked up the idea of sabbatical leaves for workers on a trip to Australia. This was mentioned by him at the convention, but at the time it seemed to be merely a long-range goal.

It was clear, however, that the union would seek to shorten the work year. Marvin Miller pointed out that vacations and holidays already averaged 200 hours a year. This came to 4 hours a week, said Miller, and it was just as meaningful as time subtracted at short intervals. "After all, if you reduce hours of work by the year, you create additional job opportunities."

The contract reopening provision gave plenty of latitude for dealing with the vacation question, as well as with a wide range of job security measures. All matters referred to the Human Relations Committee could be brought up in bargaining. The committee's assignments included sub-contracting, overtime scheduling, work by supervisors, and vacations.

"Our union is determined to expand this vacation program," said Dave McDonald. There was no hint of political dissention at the Miami meeting. McDonald was hailed by key union officials. ". . . the true members of the United Steelworkers are with him . . . ," said Joseph Germano, director of the USWA Chicago district. ". . . and he had done an excellent job. . . ." Dave McDonald seemed to be firmly in control. Moreover, it quickly turned out that McDonald's pet project—the sabbatical leave—was not just a futuristic dream.

After the convention, Steelworker officials stayed on in Miami to negotiate with the big container companies—American Can Co. and Continental Can Co. From these talks came an agreement that gave senior workers 13 weeks off every 5 years. Can-making is a fairly seasonal operation. Its slack periods meant the leaves could be granted without undue disruption.

Nevertheless, the quick agreement indicated the cost of the sabbatical plan was not as great as expected. It remained to be seen how the steel industry would price the program but it did look as though a flashy and significant labor benefit could be provided at reasonable cost to the companies. Also on the promising side for management was the move of Arthur Goldberg from the Labor Department to the Supreme Court. Goldberg was greatly respected by steel people. At the height of the 1959 bitterness, R. Heath Larry of U. S. Steel congratulated him on a brilliant argument against the Taft-Hartley injunction. One steel lawyer said Goldberg was the finest advocate in the country.

But Goldberg was closely associated with the policy of government intervention. With his dynamic makeup and his past involvement, it probably would have been impossible for him to stay out of labor disputes—particularly steel labor disputes. Succeeding Goldberg as Secretary of Labor was W. Willard Wirtz. A former law partner of Adlai Stevenson, Wirtz had served on the Board of Economic Warfare during World War II. Later he was chairman of the War Stabilization Board and a member of the War Labor Board.

Wirtz had taught law at Northwestern University before and after World War II. He fully approved of the Goldberg philosophy of defining and asserting the public interest. "I should find it the finest compliment if no one noticed the difference," he said when he took over from the retiring Secretary. But it was clear the passing of Arthur Goldberg would automatically tone down federal intervention.

Other minor factors included the acceptance September 28 of no-contest pleas from individuals in the steel forgings price fix. It did not appear the government was out to extract the last pound of flesh. A no-contest plea does not constitute an admission of guilt for civil damage suits. If individuals and companies are found guilty in criminal actions, this point is already established in suits for triple damages.

On October 2, Kaiser Steel Corp. eliminated the west coast differential by cutting prices $12 a ton. "This long-range policy is designed to spur the economy of the fast growing Western states," said Edgar F. Kaiser, company chairman. "Our schedule of prices will be revised so that we will remain competitive," said U. S. Steel. On October 4, U. S. Steel extended the cuts to galvanized sheet, wire rod, bar, and a few other products not made or not changed by Kaiser.

Elimination of the west coast premium reflected spreading competition. With slackened demand, eastern mills were reaching out further for business. One-third of Jones & Laughlin's tinplate had been going to the West Coast. A quirk in the freight rates made it less expensive to ship steel from Pittsburgh to the West Coast than from Pittsburgh to Chicago. Midwestern producers could ship to the Coast by absorbing $15 a ton in freight cost.

Competitive pressures had broken down the last big regional wall in the country. More important, national walls were crumbling. World steel production had risen from under 300 million tons in 1955 to nearly 400 million tons in 1962. The buildup of capacity abroad had cut into this country's export market. U. S. steel exports were 4 million tons in 1955, 4.3 million tons in 1956 and 5.3 million in 1957. By 1962, exports were down to 2 million tons.

Imports had been running around 1 or 1.5 million tons before 1959. In the strike year, they jumped to 4.3 million tons. Tonnage was down in 1960 and again in 1961. In 1962, with another period of labor uncertainty, imports rose to 4.1 million tons. The West Coast was particularly hard hit. It was an open target for Japan, which had tripled its steel production since 1955. This influx doubtlessly helped Kaiser decide it could not afford premium prices.

But Senator Kefauver thought otherwise. "The action proves the correctness of the position which we have held for several years that the price of steel is too high." It did not matter to the Senator that in most parts of the country, steel had already been selling at the new reduced levels of Kaiser. He suggested the change proved profits had been excessive even though Kaiser lost more than $5 million in 1962.

Two days after the price move, a complaint against the dumping of foreign rod was filed by Bethlehem, Republic, Armco, Jones & Laughlin, and two other mills. The dumping law says a country can't sell products abroad at a lower price than it charges at home. There had been complaints on wire mesh and a few other steel items earlier but the October 4 case was the first major effort in this direction.

The mills said foreign rod had taken over 30 per cent of the American market. They said imported rod was being dumped and they indicated the same thing was happening in other product lines. The mills had raised the dumping question in a serious way only a few months before. On August 16, the first full disclosure came from Henry J. Wallace, then President of U. S. Steel's National Tube Division.

"We have no blanket objection to foreign competition," said Wallace. "We've never asked for protection. We feel we are part of the world steel industry and must compete in it. But I feel in the case of buttweld pipe, we are up against a type of price competition where we're not on an even basis. West Germany is the largest shipper of buttweld pipe into the United States. A distributor in Houston is able to buy pipe from West Germany at as much as 25 per cent under our delivered prices. When you deduct transportation duties and other expense, it appears that the German producer's net return at the mill is very much lower than the net on pipe he ships to home distributors."

Wallace argued that American mills could not deal directly with import competition. "We're almost helpless to meet it. The West German producer can sell his product over here and not affect prices in his local market. If we decided we had to meet the West German price, we would be forced to reduce our entire price structure in the United States. And they could still go lower." Spot cuts, he said, "would be in conflict with our marketing methods and would completely disrupt our distribution system."

Wallace estimated imported pipe had taken over 75 per cent of the Los Angeles market and 90 per cent of the

77

Houston market. He said National Tube's buttweld mills would be operating 30 per cent higher if it were not for imports. Going down the drain, he said, was a total market of 2.8 million tons or $500 million.

At first glance, it seemed that American mills were reacting in a noncompetitive, protectionist manner to the foreign challenge. Foreign steel men jumped on this point, saying that while the Kennedy Administration was working for global unity the American steel industry was taking a step backward toward isolationism.

However, steel people argued that the question was more complicated. On the surface, they said, the foreigners might appear to represent free-wheeling competition. But in reality, it was contended, their system depended on a careful restraining of competition at home. By various cartel arrangements, it was charged, prices were being held up in Europe. The extra profits there were used to subsidize low-priced exports. Far from representing a global view, said steel men, this was a narrow approach that disregarded the damage to foreign markets while sealing off the homeland. It was not unlike the old trust concept of preying on isolated competitors while making customers in other areas foot the bill.

The American system was defended as being based on one fair price to all customers, big and small, foreign and domestic. Henry J. Wallace made one prophetic comment at this time. "They could never exist if their whole net was the same as their net on pipe sold here. But the important thing is that they feel they must have the same prices (as ours) at home in order to stay in business." Later events would show Wallace knew what he was talking about. Unfortunately for the mills, they were unable to sell their views either to the government or to foreign producers. The dumping complaints were doomed before they started.

At this point there were a few familiar echos. At an

October 19 meeting of the Business Council, Roger Blough said the economy "would be at higher levels today if the steel price increase had stuck." The next day CEA Chairman Walter Heller came back with the assertion that not all members of the business group shared Blough's view. A check of members, he said, would show that Blough had "overstated" effects of the price reversal.

On October 25 Allegheny Ludlum put some teeth in its earlier tightening of discounts by dropping base prices of stainless sheets 5 per cent. Other mills had not followed when Allegheny went to lower allowances in June; distributors had continued to pass along commissions. Now, with the whole structure lower, any extra discounts would really come out of the hides of the producers. "With a cut like that, you have to follow," said J. M. Curley, chairman of Eastern Stainless Steel Corp. "Producers can now at least quote a price that is even with the distributors," said T. S. Fitch, president of Washington Steel Corp.

In stainless steel, price pressure was giving technology an extra forward push. Washington Steel was changing to pressure casting. Allegheny Ludlum was experimenting with the oxygen process and direct reduction. The mills were also modifying their products in many different ways. To overcome corrosion on auto stripping, Allegheny Ludlum went to bright annealing—a method in which the metal was heated in an inert atmosphere. For the same problem, Allegheny added copper to the straight-chrome 430 grade being used. Then some other producer added molybdenum. For special auto applications, columbium was added.

All the special alloys and processes were introduced and used without price changes. In the fight to beat corrosion and aluminum, the mills then started working on completely new grades. Entirely apart from this, sheet and plate prices were being knocked down by the fight with distributors. And special concessions were being made on the grades most susceptible to import competition. It was a pretty chaotic situation. Some of the price cutting made no sense but the whole process did have meaning.

"From 1940 to 1957," said William B. Pierce, sales vice-president of Allegheny Ludlum, "we had a sellers' market. It was pretty difficult to make a mistake. After 1957, demand flattened out. At the same time supply increased. With a great excess of supply, the price structure collapsed of its own weight. Prices sought a level that would increase demand and reduce supply. One element in price reductions has been a move to maintain and expand markets."

The price reductions apparently did produce growth. Allegheny Ludlum stainless prices dropped 25 per cent from 1958 to 1965. But from 1956, the company's sales volume rose 52 per cent. In roughly the same period, prices of all steel products rose 26 per cent while total shipments went up less than 10 per cent. Some experts argue that steel has priced itself out of some markets.

The mills reply, first of all, that the question is academic. With the industry averaging less than 6 per cent on sales in 1961, the price level could not have been appreciably lower without eliminating profits altogether. Moreover, steel officials argued that cutting prices did not increase sales. The slogan was: "Nobody gains in a price cut."

The closing days of the year saw two contradictory omens. A number of statements by Walter Heller at that time were interpreted as opening the door for selective price hikes. Heller seemed to be saying the guideline concept did not envision a rigid ceiling of prices. At the same time, however, seven steel officials were summoned to appear before the New York grand jury that was digging into prices. Many people thought this probe had been dropped and the new call came as a disquieting jolt.

80

1963 · THE ROAD BACK

If ever an industry needed a quiet, peaceful labor settlement, it was basic steel in 1963. But the industry went into the year with all signs pointing to strenuous negotiations. From this starting position, the outlook became worse.

The year 1963 began in an inauspicious manner. On January 3, Crucible Steel cut 1½¢ from the price of type 301 strip. This was part of the running fight with Allegheny Ludlum. It put the 301 grade on a price par with 201. On February 19, U. S. Steel reduced 301 strip by 2.75¢. Two days later, Allegheny Ludlum came back and cut the 201 by 3.75¢. This sequence had the effect of leaving stainless grades containing nickel priced below some grades that contained no nickel.

Meanwhile, steel people were glum about the whole price outlook. On January 9, Arthur B. Homer, Bethlehem chairman, said it "was not time for a price increase. We ought to be trying to get a price increase but we can't do that without putting ourselves out of business." Homer urged a cut in wages. Crucible Steel president Joel Hunter talked along the same lines. "I would hope that over the long pull we would get our costs down and that this would be translated into price reductions."

On February 18, A. S. Glossbrenner, president of Youngstown Sheet & Tube Co., felt it was "hard to visualize any significant increases no matter how justified they may be from a cost-price standpoint." On February 28, U. S. Steel offered users delayed billing on tinplate. This arrangement provided that users could build inventory if labor contracts were reopened but would not have to pay for it until used. Clad plate prices were cut 10 per cent by Lukens Steel on March 22.

On April 2, U. S. Steel, Bethlehem Steel, Armco, and three others were indicted for fixing prices of wrought steel wheels. It was charged the companies met in such high-class surroundings as the Yale Club in New York and the Duquesne Club in Pittsburgh. There, they allegedly agreed to maintain identical list prices and to correct any "mistakes" in bidding. By mistakes was meant "non-identical delivered prices to a customer as a result of a mathematical error." A separate indictment charged a number of smaller companies with fixing prices on steel pipe flanges and rings.

In Des Moines, Iowa, on April 8, Roger Blough addressed the Iowa Medical Society. "No one in Government —no matter how highly placed—should interfere with the business decisions of our people." He discussed the profit problems of the industry and added: "If rising wages bring higher production costs, must not rising prices inevitably follow?"

The same thought had occurred to William A. Steele, president of Wheeling Steel Corp. While Blough was talking in Des Moines, Steele was noting that profits were at a "dangerous minimum." He said he intended to do something about this "when feasible."

The next day—April 9—Arthur Homer was adding to his company's reputation for timely comments. "There's considerable doubt in my mind as to whether the market will support a price increase. . . ." Allison Maxwell of Pittsburgh Steel said there was "no question about the justification of higher prices." A few hours later, Wheeling Steel announced a $6 a ton increase in plate and sheet products. "A steady increase in costs of materials, services and labor, with no increase in steel prices since 1958, prompted today's action."

The effective date of the increase—April 10—was just 1 year after the 1962 explosion. This day in 1963 found steel leaders in the unhappy position of meeting together behind closed doors. The 35-man board of the American Iron & Steel Institute was holding a scheduled session in New York. Present were the heads of mills that were about to make their separate and independent decisions on the price increase. "It's a tough racket, boys," said A. S. Glossbrenner of Youngstown as he emerged from the meeting. "It's a rat race." Tom Patton of Republic said his only knowledge of the price move was "what I read in the papers." There was a long pause as the industry waited for a reaction from President Kennedy. It was fairly certain there would not be another explosion.

Unlike the 1962 move, Wheeling's increase was selective. It covered slightly under half their total line of steel products. Walter Heller had hinted there was room for selective increases in the Administration's scheme. Moreover, the new hike was being made before a labor settlement rather than after. Finally, the backwash of opinion from the 1962 outburst left most people with the feeling that a display of federal moderation was in order.

"Administration intervention now would be difficult to justify," said the *New York Times*. "Along with many other steel producers, Wheeling has been suffering a profit
83

squeeze, so much so that it cut its dividend last year. . . . The market place is a powerful and impartial judge," concluded the *Times*.

Steel profits had certainly not surged upward in the manner predicted by government economists. The American Iron & Steel Institute reported a drop in steel earnings from $689 million in 1961 to $566 million in 1962. The Institute said 1962 profits were the lowest since 1938. Although a portion of the profit drops can be attributed to changes in the tax laws allowing a lower reported income proportional to actual cash flow, the industry was not getting rich. It earned only 4 per cent on sales in 1962. It didn't seem to be getting the added volume the Administration had promised.

There was one other point considered significant by steel legal men. The general grand jury investigation of the 1962 price hike had been allowed to lapse. The jury had recessed. The key witnesses had not been called. One trust lawyer considered this a definite peace offering.

On Thursday at 2 P.M., President Kennedy had his say. He was still against across-the-board increases. "I opposed such an increase last year. I oppose it now." But he said, "I realize that selected price adjustments up or down as prompted by changes in supply or demand—as opposed to across-the-board increases—are not incompatible with a framework of general stability. . . ."

There was more but this much was enough for steel people. Without unseemly haste, they lined up behind the increases. On Monday, Republic was the first of the big ones to follow. It's increase of $5.34 a ton on sheet was slightly under the $5.50 of Wheeling. Pittsburgh Steel put through the full Wheeling increase. On April 16, Armco went up on both sheet and plate but cut wire prices $5 a ton. U. S. Steel then came out with increases averaging $4.85 a ton. It did not include plate. The one remaining question was disposed of when Inland Steel followed. "These price increases are well justified by market conditions and unsatisfactory profit margins," said Inland.

The *Times* called the divergence of the mills in their increases "most unusual." Some purchasing agents were cynical on this point. They noted that Wheeling, which did not have a plate mill, had increased plate prices. This, they said, permitted the other mills to display their competitive instincts by knocking down part of the increase. The whole untidy action did suggest the mills were bending over backwards in an effort to be nonuniform in their price changes.

Nevertheless, the big breakthrough had been pulled off fairly smoothly. In the industry and possibly in the Administration, people were relieved to have the curse removed, the tension eased and the precedent of intervention weakened. When all the dust had settled, the increase covered 41 per cent of steel tonnage and 29 per cent of its dollar sales. On the products affected, the increase came to $4.95 a ton or 3.42 per cent. On all products, it amounted to a little under 1 per cent.

The difficulty was that the increase helped some mills more than others and some not at all. This point was noted by William G. Stewart, president of Universal-Cyclops Steel Corp. Stewart parodied the President's 1962 words, arguing that wage increases should also be selective. "Remember, any across-the-board wage increase will injure the public interest," he said. The important part of his comments was the suggestion that mills might not be finished with price increases.

There were a few mild rumbles in Washington. Senator Paul H. Douglas (D., Ill.) announced steel price hearings of the Congressional Joint Economic Committee for the following week. Senator Mike Mansfield (D., Mont.) called for industry statesmanship "of the highest order." But Senator Goldwater called the President's action "enlightened." There was no desire for a confrontation in Washington or in Palm Beach, where the President was staying. On April 19, Mr. Kennedy said the companies had acted with "some restraint."

The President appealed to the steel union to "conduct itself in accord with its long-range interest, which is the national interest. Price stability is the best thing for the steel industry and wage stability is the best thing for the steel union." The President feared that "the psychological effect may cause a more general rise in prices which may therefore be reflected in additional wage demands."

The Wheeling increase had come only a few weeks before May 1, the date on which steel-labor contracts could be reopened by the steel union. Reports from the bargaining had not been encouraging to start with. The price move seemed to make a dogfight certain. The two sides had been bargaining since January 17 within the Human Relations Committee. At the beginning of the bargaining, one union official cautioned against expecting quick results. "Although the talks are being given a big buildup, I frankly think it will be quite a while before we get beyond the routine stage."

For a long time, it didn't look as though talks would ever get beyond the routine stage. The government was issuing a few general promptings. On February 19, Willard Wirtz expressed "considerable confidence that the situation would be worked out without a major disruption." With Arthur Goldberg gone, however, and with the memory of last year's mess still vivid, the Administration was avoiding any detailed involvement.

Meanwhile, pressures were building up on the negotiators. In late April, word came that the Steelworkers had gotten a fat payment under the sharing plan of Kaiser Steel. This was a program that protected workers against job

86

loss due to technical displacement and offered them one-third of any direct production savings.

The preliminary word on the sharing plan had come December 16 after a Washington meeting of Edgar Kaiser and President Kennedy. At that time, steel men had registered dismay and distrust. "I don't think productivity per se should be used as a guideline," said Avery Adams, Jones & Laughlin chairman. He pointed out that cost cuts usually resulted from new investments. "This industry cannot afford another employment cost increase," said Adams.

A steel financial man pointed out that Kaiser, with its modern plant, figured to make a good cost showing. But with its big debt, the company might still be operating in the red. "They damn well could be giving out increases when they're losing money—and this is something." That was one of the basic industry objections to all guidelines. Output per man-hour was not a measure of total productivity, the mills contended. Unless you considered total input—including investment and raw material—you had no measure of real productivity. Apart from the principle and the cost, steel people didn't see how you could devise a plan that would compensate for volume changes and buying shifts.

These doubts were not eased in late April when it was announced that in the first month of the plan, eligible Kaiser employees had gotten a payoff of more than $300,-000, or 55¢ an hour for those participating.

Two days before—on April 23—Leon Greenberg of the Bureau of Labor Statistics had testified before the Joint Economic Committee that there had been practically no increase in unit labor costs of the steel industry in recent years. From 1958 to 1962, the unit cost rose only 0.6 per cent a year, said Greenberg. This compared with an annual average of 4.6 per cent since 1947, he added.

87

A few weeks before, the mills had raised prices. On April 25, Arthur Homer had maintained that the increase was "not sufficient to allow higher labor demands." Avery Adams of Jones & Laughlin agreed. "It seems obvious that . . . all concerned would be best served by holding employment cost at the present high level." Right on top of these statements came the word that Kaiser was raising pay 55¢ an hour.

Everything pointed to a tough labor stand with full-dress bargaining. To make matters worse, Dave McDonald came down with what was described as a routine virus infection. McDonald had left talks to rest in his California home. There were all sorts of dark rumors about a much more serious illness.

However, a few hopeful notes were sounded. The Kaiser payment was put in perspective by Dr. George W. Taylor, who was one of the public members of the tripartite committee set up in 1959. "It's about what you'd expect," said Taylor. "This is a program for putting non-incentive workers on incentive. You figure what incentive rates are in the rest of the industry—20 to 30 per cent—and it's about what you'd expect."

In February, the plan had been discussed by Marvin Miller, the Steelworkers' staff man who really put it together. "You're not giving more," said Miller. "You're creating more. If you leave out the minimum guarantee, the only circumstance in which the worker gets more is when the company gets more."

"When you pick this thing apart, you start to lose some of the flavor." Miller recalled the management charges of featherbedding in 1959. "Insofar as an employee affects production and production efficiency, it seems the height of absurdity to say I want you to be more efficient when the net effect is to lose your job."

"We've tried to see what happens when you say that no matter what happens technologically, you will not lose your job and you will get a share in the gains. You can't compare this with the best of all worlds. You must compare before and after." Kaiser could still be losing money "but if direct unit costs are reduced, it will be better off after than before. If the plan works the way we expect it to, then the rest of the industry will have a hard time arguing against it."

These comments brought out, among other things, the strong feeling within the Steelworkers that bargaining and all labor relations could be put on a more objective basis. The Kaiser plan was an effort to automate the business of dividing the pie. In talks with the rest of the industry, the union was also seeking to find a more rational substitute for the usual power play. The industry was thinking along these lines but it was the union that had the big decision to make. If it served a reopening notice May 1, there would be another strike deadline, another crisis, and another grinding test of wills.

Dave McDonald is credited with keeping his people in line and avoiding the crisis. He returned from the desert in good shape. As May 1 approached, the feeling of pessimism and inaction gradually faded. "I am hopeful that all the crisis atmosphere that accompanies a reopening can be avoided," said Roger Blough on April 30. At the time, he was reporting that U. S. Steel's first quarter earnings were the worst since 1948.

In Pittsburgh, Dave McDonald said no decision had been made on a reopening of contracts. Since the union's wage-policy committee had not been summoned, it was evident there would not be a strike notice May 1. On the official day—May 1—McDonald told a business symposium, "There may be no need for a formal contract reopening."

He said the Human Relations Committee was making "a lot of progress. We must not be selfish. We must look beyond our own desires."

This forebearance was to prove costly the next year. McDonald later insisted that I. W. Abel, who was then secretary-treasurer of the Steelworkers, had favored a settlement on very nominal terms. Abel denied this. Another union man said Abel was anxious to avoid government intervention on the grounds that it would be impossible to settle local problems. A company bargainer said the only impression he had was that Abel was bored with the lengthy proceedings.

After May 1, the strike threat faded but it didn't seem there was very rapid movement in bargaining positions. The companies winced when they looked at first quarter earnings. U. S. Steel was down 47 per cent. Bethlehem was off 50 per cent. Republic reported a 37 per cent drop from 1962. Tom Patton of Republic said further increases of employment costs would be a "telling blow."

"If we increase employment costs, it will be that much worse," said A. S. Glossbrenner of Youngstown Sheet & Tube. But on May 14, Dave McDonald indicated that the union was willing to keep talking. "As long as the Human Relations Committee is at work, I'm satisfied." On May 22, Logan T. Johnston of Armco Steel Corp. was "encouraged by recent developments." Roger Blough said the Human Relations work was "on the encouraging side." Charles M. Beeghly of Jones & Laughlin detected an "improvement in the labor picture."

Tom Patton commented on the "constructive approach" of avoiding a crisis. Reports from the bargainers were vague. "The cards are not on the table," said one company official. But he added this. "The fact you've got to remember is that both sides want the Human Relations idea to work. And if there is a reopener, the whole thing is down the drain." What they were trying to achieve was the open-end bargaining of the coal industry. Under this arrangement, the coal people had gone for more than 10 years without a general strike, without formal bargaining, and without price increases.

At irregular intervals, the operators and the coal union would meet informally and work out new terms. The privacy and informality of this method was considered good by both sides. "Labor leaders who state demands publicly have a tough time backtracking," said Edward G. Fox, president of the Bituminous Coal Operators' Assn. "Men tend to think in terms of what they didn't get. Gains don't look so big."

Fox noted that the coal industry had gotten away from the inventory surges that had once been so disruptive. On the other side, the union felt there was an advantage in being able to pick its spots. "The Mineworkers have had the advantage of being able to move when the economic climate is favorable," said Joseph Yablonski, president, United Mine Workers, District 5.

This was the kind of flexibility the steel bargainers were trying desperately to achieve. With one early settlement in 1962, it was felt that if they could just get through this session without fireworks, they would prove to users, the government, and themselves that steel contracts could be negotiated in an orderly manner.

This was the goal but it wasn't coming easy. A union official called it "the craziest bargaining I've ever seen." Talks had reached the negotiation stage, he said, but they were still being conducted under rules designed for study and exploration. There was constant backtracking, he said, as concessions in one area would bring new arguments in another. There was no orderly progression; both sides were free to reverse themselves on any point. This was part of the Human Relations philosophy. Bargainers were to be free to explore without being committed. The idea was to promote open exchanges and get away from the guarded, rigid type of bargaining that had failed so often in the past.

The union source said there would be a peaceful settlement, however. Others were now concluding the same thing. Details of the agreement were oozing out. Frequently, a labor agreement will be reached in a big dramatic jump. There will be reports of a stalemate, of a large gap, and then suddenly there will be an important move and the thing will be settled. It didn't happen that way in 1963. It took a week or more after the essentials had been negotiated before all the nagging details had been nailed down.

Finally, on June 20, came the official announcement that a contract costing 15¢ over 21 months had been signed. The main provision was the sabbatical leave plan of Dave McDonald. The senior half of the work force would get 13 weeks off every 5 years. There was a tentative agreement on subcontracting. There were various other job protection measures. Medical and insurance benefits were increased. But the big benefit was the extended leave. Dave McDonald estimated this would create 20,000 new jobs in basic steel. From the companies' standpoint, the beauty of the contract was its cost. The 15¢ package came to about 9¢ a year or 2 per cent a year. This was the lowest cost increase in the postwar period.

Company officials felt compelled to gripe a little about disruptive effects of long vacations. "What hidden cost in the form of lower efficiency will follow is unknown," said Charles Beeghly of Jones & Laughlin. Privately, steel men had to admit they had done pretty well. "There's no price increase in this," said one staff man.

Even more important than the terms, however, was the manner in which the contract had been negotiated. "The idea was to remove our problems from the critical pressures of contract deadlines," said Dave McDonald, "and at the same time, reduce or eliminate the boom or bust cycle which such deadlines generate. We have accomplished that purpose and by so doing, we are perhaps one step closer to realization of the end of industrial strikes in the steel industry."

McDonald hailed the contributions of the Human Relations Committee. He stressed that there had been no federal intervention. "We sought no aid and none was proffered." The White House said the President was gratified. The *Times* news story said steel labor relations had "passed into a new era of accommodation."

R. Conrad Cooper and Heath Larry of U. S. Steel later gave a detailed analysis of the Human Relations philosophy. "Somehow or other it has come to be recognized by both sides that equity and understanding must play a greater part in labor relations." said Larry. "The trouble in 1959," said Cooper, "was that there was little real bargaining. Hard positions had been taken on both sides, and reason had less influence than the threats of, and use of, economic force." After the strike, he continued, the Human Relations program was begun "with considerable trepidation." However, "the process of jointly seeking our relevant facts developed confidence."

Larry thought that "there's no room for sharpness if you have to live with people. The long abrasive process involved here tends to do away with shadow boxing." Cooper stated, "when we got close to the time for 1962 bargaining, the top committee . . . said: 'Now you have looked at the relevant information. Have you reached the point of making recommendations?' That method did bring forth the basis for good solutions."

The Human Relations meetings started right after the 1962 settlement. They went on a continuous basis January 15 and they didn't stop until actual terms had been devised. Was this bargaining or something else? "Whatever you call it, a collective bargain was made," said Larry. "An atmosphere of problem solving continued all through the Committee meetings," said Cooper. He noted that special procedures were not the important thing. "The mechanism wouldn't change things one iota in a labor management relationship where the proper will was missing."

Cooper also said the Human Relations ground rules were helpful in creating the right feeling. Before, he said, "if you recognized a point as something that had to be dealt with, you had made a concession. If you ventured a chip in the game, it was irretrievable. That in itself inhibited free and constructive discussions." Cooper said it was vital to keep talks private. "It has become important not to have anybody's free-wheeling thoughts come back to haunt him. Public position-taking tends to harden bargaining lines."

Also helpful was the idea of continuing talks. "If you have a complex problem, its full consideration takes time," said Cooper. The absence of a deadline was considered vital. With a limited amount of time, said Cooper, there was "inevitabily a crisis situation." What about next time? "We've gone through two situations and arrived at agreements twice," said Cooper. "We're encouraged by the experience with the Human Relations program. We sense the same feeling in the union."

Tending to brighten the outlook further was the provision that the new contract had a 120-day waiting period after any reopening. It appeared that this long delay would finally get rid of the inventory building that always accompanied steel labor talks. Users would have ample time after the notice to build stocks. If agreement could be reached without a formal opening, there would be no protective buying.

It did, indeed, seem that the steel industry was out from under the gun. "The new steel labor agreement," said the *Times* editorial, "represents a triumph of reason and moderation in an industry with a long record of turbulence." So

94

in the space of a few months, the industry had shaken off the pox on both its prices and its labor relations. It was a golden moment but it was too good to be true.

The steel industry was determined to press its advantage. After a spasm of relief when the April price increase stuck, steel people began having second thoughts. That one hike had not, after all, been so great. "Most of our products are still priced at 1958 levels or less despite six subsequent labor cost increases," said Tom Patton on June 21. The situation was not "a happy one." Inland Steel Chairman Joseph Block was equally unhappy. "There can be no doubt that the steel industry still needs higher prices, as well as increased volume and lower costs, to make an adequate return on invested capital."

On July 2, eight steel companies and nine executives were indicted for fixing the prices of steel castings. This was the fourth indictment since April 10 of 1962. The companies charged included Bethlehem Steel, which had been named in three previous indictments. It was alleged the companies met in the Duquesne Club and various hotels to agree on general increases, collaborate on price catalogues, and swap helpful information. It looked a little as though the government was breaking a single conspiracy into a string of actions. Erb Gurney, who had figured in the forgings case, was also named in the castings indictment. Emil H. Lang, chairman of Erie Forge Co., had also been charged in an earlier indictment. As in the forgings case, the product involved was on the fringe of the steel industry. Blaw-Knox Co., which was one of those indicted July 2, was primarily an equipment builder. The same was true of Pittsburgh Steel Foundry Co. and Birdsboro Corp.

The timing of the indictments was fortuitous from the Administration's standpoint. Whenever the industry was asserting its right to competitive freedom, one of the price-fix cases would hit the headlines. The Justice Department could hardly pull an indictment out of its hat at a strategic moment. However, it was clearly doing a thorough job of checking on the movements of steel executives.

At the time, it looked as though the steel market might do a fairly good job of policing prices. On August 15, Armco Steel reduced the price of types 302 and 304 stainless sheet by 2.75¢ a pound. These were the big general-purpose grades. Their prices had been weakened by the action on 301 earlier. Armco was restoring the traditional differential of $70 a ton. This action indicated one of the difficulties of selective price changes. Users would attempt to switch to cheaper grades. Or a producer might start to fudge alloy content, selling a better steel under a low-priced brand.

In general, though, the steel market was starting to emerge from its 5-year slump. In mid-August, *Iron Age* predicted an upturn by September. Earlier reports had called for inventory liquidation to depress mill operations for the rest of the year. Now it seemed that the liquidation period would be relatively shallow and brief. It wasn't apparent at the time, but a steady rise in the consumption of steel had started.

Possibly heartened by market reactions, the mills began trying a few price moves. In August, Inland Steel went back to published prices for reinforcing bars. The new list price was somewhat above the negotiated figures being used earlier. U. S. Steel continued to negotiate rebar prices. The classification of Inland's change was to assume some importance shortly when reporters started adding up increases.

In September, there was a clear-cut rise when Jones & Laughlin initiated a 4 per cent hike for oil-country drill pipe and casing. This restored a cut made July 13, 1961. On September 20, U. S. Steel followed with an increase on these products. The products involved came to about 2 per cent of total steel shipments.

On September 20, Youngstown Sheet & Tube announced a $5 a ton boost for hot rolled carbon bars and semifinished steel. On September 30, Republic added alloy and cold finished bars. Its increase on certain semifinished grades was only $4—$1 less than Youngstown's. A *New York Times* story recalled that the steel industry had "exhibited new finesse" in the April round.

On October 1, U. S. Steel, Jones & Laughlin, and Armco followed. At the same time, Armco cut the prices of 304 stainless sheet in standard widths. This was aimed at imports, which were concentrated in the standard sizes. The *Times,* with a straight face, commented again on the nonuniformity of the increases. "There appears to be considerable divergence in assessments of present market strength."

By October 2, the new increases totaled 8 to 12 per cent of the market—depending on how you classified rebars. This brought the percentage since April 10 somewhere around 50 per cent. The speculation in Washington was that anything over 75 per cent would be considered an across-the-board increase. On October 2, Bethlehem threw in a $5 a ton increase for carbon plate. Inland added structurals. These two amounted to 15 per cent of steel shipments. They brought the cumulative increase to between 65 and 70 per cent. The Administration was silent.

On October 3, U. S. Steel followed on plate and upped the ante on large line pipe (24 to 36 in.) by $7 a ton. Lukens Steel boosted alloy plate $7 a ton. It was brought out that Armco was attempting to cut the jobber discount on 304 sheet. (A lower discount meant a higher price charged by the mill.)

At this point, the increases came close to the magic number of 75 per cent. Washington sources said the Administration was unhappy but that no outburst was expected. The cumulative hike was estimated as 3½ per cent of affected products and 2 per cent of all products. At

97

his press conference October 9, the President talked mostly about the $250 million sale of wheat to Russia. Asked about steel prices, his comments were restrained. "For the time being, we are watching the matter with concern and will continue in the days ahead to do so." He referred to high profits and the need to avoid an inflationary spiral but there was no dire warning.

Then came another bomb. On October 21, the big steel companies were subpoenaed to appear before a grand jury price probe. The mills were jolted. "This took the industry by surprise," said Republic. "The relationship between steel management and the government has been so good lately. This threw a little bit of a monkey wrench into it." The next day, steel stocks took another bath. U. S. Steel opened at 52½—down 3½. Youngstown Sheet & Tube opened 6 points down. Both stocks recovered some of the losses during the day.

Tom Patton of Republic spoke regretfully of the new turn. "I hope it is not evidence of any deteriorating of the improved relations." On October 23, a special grand jury was impaneled in a New York federal court. It was brought out that U. S. Steel, Bethlehem, Republic, and the six other biggest companies had been served subpoenas calling for personnel information going back to 1952 and price dope from January of 1956.

The products involved were sheet, strip, bar, tinplate, and plate. Only bar and plate had been involved in the most recent hike. It was evident from this and from the time span of subpoenas that the probe was directed at past moves. To steel men this looked like arbitrary retaliation for the recent increases. The 1962 hikes had already gotten a thorough going over and no evidence of wrong doing had been turned up.

The 1962 grand jury had started a broad investigation of past action. This had been cut off early in the year. The jury had recessed and was dismissed when its term expired. Records had been returned to the companies. If there had been evidence of criminal activity, it seemed strange that the broad inquiry should have been stopped. If there was no evidence, the new probe appeared to be a general witch-hunting expedition, started as a punitive measure against companies that had exercised their right to raise prices.

In the light of later events, the really puzzling question is this: Why didn't the government go after the companies sooner? The speed of the October move and its results suggest the feds had stored some interesting information for a rainy day.

1964 · ALMOST PERFECT

1964 was to be almost a perfect year for steel. There were no big swings. Demand moved up to a high level and stayed there. Moreover, steel-labor relations had finally been put on an orderly footing. It was a golden time— until things started going wrong. Little things at first and then a bomb.

The price-fix probe was quickly forgotten in early 1964. The steel industry started the year thinking it might equal 1963 production of 110 million tons. After a month or two, mill officials began to hope they might approach the records of 1955–1957 boom. Then it became clear the industry was going to have not just a good year but an almost perfect year. This was to be a year of steady high demand, not inflated by inventory building nor torpedoed by inventory liquidation.

This kind of stable, comfortable prosperity was almost unknown to the steel industry. Usually, mills were breaking their backs trying to provide users with extra inventory or flat on their backs while customers worked off surplus stock. The inventory cycle tended to accentuate the business cycle for steel. In the opinion of some economists, inventory swings were the main cause of general economic fluctuations. And the unstable labor situation was seen as the cause of the inventory excesses.

On March 27, the *New York Times* reported the "dramatic emergence from Wall Street's doghouse" of steel stocks. The turnabout had come in 1963. Now, U. S. Steel, Bethlehem, Republic, and other big ones were hitting new highs for the years. On April 8, the plug was pulled out. The grand jury convened in October returned price-fixing indictments against U. S. Steel, Bethlehem Steel, National Steel, Republic, Jones & Laughlin, Armco, and Wheeling.

The companies were charged with meeting in New York's Biltmore and Sheraton East hotels. The products involved were hot rolled, cold rolled, and galvanized sheet. These were not fringe items; they were the bread-and-butter products of tonnage mills. The government said the market for the products named was worth $3.6 billion, or one-third of total steel sales. Sales of the defendant companies were estimated at $2 billion a year.

Only two individuals were charged but they were big ones. William J. Stephens was then president of Jones & Laughlin. He had been a sales executive with Bethlehem at the time of the alleged collusion. Stephens was a roly-poly individual who had been with Bethlehem for 39 years before coming to Jones & Laughlin to fill a vacancy in the top echelon.

Barton was in charge of sheet products at U. S. Steel. Born in Frazer, Minnesota, he had studied electrical engineering at the University of Minnesota and worked in the electrical industry before joining U. S. Steel in 1935. In 1952, he became manager of sheet and strip products. Barton was a strong-looking, strong-talking man, well over 6 feet tall, with the jaw of a Marine and a vocabulary that could rattle partitions in the U. S. Steel building. People moved when he raised his voice at U. S. Steel. When he said "No," even the most extensive programs stopped. "Doesn't U. S. Steel hire anyone under 6 feet," asked one visitor after meeting Barton. He was possibly the old-style steelmaster—the kind of guy people expected to see when Roger Blough appeared on TV screens at the 1962 press conference.

At any rate, the indictment named two key executives— Barton and Stephens—along with seven major mills. Several other companies were identified as conspirators but were not indicted. This was the seventh such case since April 10, 1962. The forgings case broke April 26 of 1962. After that came wrought wheels on April 2 of 1963 and pipe flanges the same day. On February 10, 1964, U. S. Steel was involved in a regional case on structural steel. On March 10, 1964, U. S. Steel and Kaiser were indicted for rigging water pipe prices in 10 Western states.

It could not be said the mills had looked good. And now the sheet case reached into the heart of the industry. This was no peripheral thing. The mills were charged with top-level price rigging in their most important product lines. The allegations "strike at basic and cherished principles of American business," said the *Times* editorial of April 9. If there has been fixing, "the steel industry will have done untold damage to itself and to the ground rules that have governed competition." The industry was making "a myth of its own principles."

The steel people did the best they could to muster a reply. Republic "regretted that defense of these unjustifiable charges will consume a great deal of the effort of our management at a time when all its attention should be devoted to the important economic problems facing us today." Edmund F. Martin, vice-chairman of Bethlehem, noted that the government had gone "back in the fifties,"

102

to drag out "ancient history." "Even assuming that the matters charged were true, the Department of Justice is seeking not to correct any illegal or improper present-day situation but only to harrass the industry for practices which even under the allegation of the indictment have been abandoned."

Republic, U. S. Steel, Jones & Laughlin, and Armco vigorously denied the charges. A National Steel spokesman said the company had nothing to say. Did this mean, no comment? No, he was not authorized to say "No comment." Later, he called back and said, "No comment." U. S. Steel made the point that only extras and not base prices were involved. Since extras were only one-sixth of the whole price, it said, the sales figure was $320 million and not $2 billion.

One interpretation, by a *Times* news writer, was that the fixing charges blasted the theory the mills could keep prices up by "administering." Gardiner Means, author of the administered price concept, took exception to this in an April 13 letter. "The indictments . . . were solely concerned with extras. . . ." he argued. This was only a small fraction of the total cost. "Nearly all the rise in steel prices from 1953 to 1958 . . . was the rise in base prices and could not possibly be explained by collusion in the setting of the amounts to be charged for extras." In an administered industry, "a price can be set for a period of time and a series of transactions . . . it stands in the way of automatic adjustments on which our society classically relied."

Purchasing agents have long regarded the extra system as a device for putting through quiet price increases. In 1958, the system had been defended by Richard F. Sentner, executive vice-president, commercial, U. S. Steel. "Extras are a method for calculating prices for particular specifications. They are added to a price base to give a charge that will accurately reflect the cost of processing an individual order. The term 'extra' is misleading; it's actually an integral part of the overall net price of an order for a particular steel. . . . The extra system gives a customer the chance to evaluate the cost of a particular requirement."

Another point was discussed privately by steel men. The indictment, they said, related in part to putting standards on an orderly basis. This was something the government had urged steel people and others to do in World War II. The whole area dealt essentially with the business of defining standards. Should a company charge an extra for drawing quality? Should there be a higher charge for a trimmed edge? How much working should a commercial quality sheet take? These questions involved money but they also involved order. The user had to know what kind of steel he was getting. The producer had to know what quality level was needed.

But beyond this, there was the old question of whether price disorder—price competition—should not be restrained before it reaches the destructive point. It was all very good for Gardiner Means to admire the free swings of wheat and other commodity prices. Steel men argued that in a mass-production industry, the inflexibility of costs could not be ignored. Neither, said the mills, could the inflexible demands of a strong labor organization.

The industry had been through the wringer on this question. Fifty or 60 years ago, steel prices were quoted on a daily basis. That was before continuous strip mills and 400-ton open hearths. In the thirties, price discipline had broken down. But that was before the big industrial unions moved in. Steel had had its sweatshop phase, its jobshop phase, and its speculative phase. By World War II, it was a mature industry, knowledgeable in the commercial and financial implications of mass production. And if there was one thing the mills understood, it was that cost was the base —the Bible.

Cost floors could not be disregarded because business was bad. And neither should they be disregarded when business was good. Steel prices did not come tumbling down in slumps partly because they never went up. There was no speculation by mills in boom periods. Steel was never auctioned off to the highest bidders. But granting all these things, should there be such uniformity in steel pricing? Shouldn't some mills have lower costs than others? One steel answer might be that even the most efficient and profitable companies haven't made enough money. Inland Steel, for example, has been one of the most insistent complainers about inadequate earnings.

Apart from this, there is the practical fact, recognized by Judge Gary years ago, that some degree of self-regulation was necessary in a big, conspicuous industry. This point was brought out vividly in the summer of 1961 when the Justice Department was wrapping up price-fixing cases in the electrical industry. The companies were asked to sign a consent decree binding them to avoid unreasonably *low* prices. The decree stipulated economic effects could be the standard in judging behavior.

Westinghouse Electric Corp. and three others went along with the government. General Electric resisted. "Even with the government condoning it, we're not going to get involved in price-fixing," said GE chairman Ralph J. Cordiner. Cordiner said the decree would force GE to sell at the price of its least efficient competitor. Other company officials said the order was vague, that a company could only comply by asking the government what price to charge.

It seemed strange that after nailing the electrical people for conspiring to hold prices up, the Justice Department should propose a remedy that forbade excessive price-cutting. Actually, the case merely highlighted a basic conflict. An industry can get into trouble by not being competitive enough. For the electrical companies, this was a matter of actual collusion. In the steel and auto industries, orderly pricing has attracted suspicion and criticism. But as Judge Gary understood, a company can also get in hot water by being too competitive and too successful. There are specific laws prohibiting predatory pricing and price discrimination.

The theory is that a big predator can destroy competition by pricing without regard to costs in a certain area or product line. Likewise the big customer can secure price concessions that give it a discriminatory advantage over competitors. In theory, a General Motors or a U. S. Steel may destroy some competitors—without predatory practices —on the basis of lower costs. This honest victory is theoretically applauded.

"The successful competitor, having been urged to compete, must not be turned upon when he wins," said Judge Learned Hand, in a 1945 trust case involving Aluminum Company of America. But if a company keeps winning until there is no competition left, it becomes a monopoly. If this happens or comes close to happening, the company is turned on by the government.

There is a real squeeze in this situation. During the Eisenhower Administration, there was conflict between the antitrust division under Robert Bicks and the Federal Trade Commission under Earl W. Kinter. While Bicks was bugging companies to cut prices, Kinter was after them for being too flexible in their pricing. During the long period of aluminum price weakness, Alcoa salesmen complained that they were losing orders because the company required written documentation before it would meet a competitive cut.

In the electrical industry at the time of the consent decree, TVA and other government agencies were buying foreign equipment and complaining about identical domestic prices. At the same time, the Justice Department was warning against too much price-cutting. Lee Loevinger, who headed the antitrust division at the time, insisted the difficulties were exaggerated—that between the extremes of predatory pricing and price-fixing there was a big middle ground for healthy competition. "They haven't ruined the game of football because you can't gouge or knee," he said. "The entire bar has yet to come up with a case where a company was ruined because of laws governing pricing."

But why were the electrical companies enjoined from cutting prices after a conspiracy to hold prices up? "The electrical companies were not convicted of holding prices up," said Loevinger. "They were convicted of fixing prices by illegal means. The Justice Department is not concerned whether prices are high or low. It is concerned only that no illegal means, collusive or predatory, be used in pricing."

Loevinger went on to say the consent decree simply made it a little easier to enforce the law. Its provisions did not really go beyond the law, he argued. "How do you ever show predatory intent except by showing economic effects?" This was possibly the nub of industry's problem: economic concentration tends to be equated with monopolistic motives. Justice Department people did not feel GE was being made the victim of an economic accident. A ban against unreasonable cutting was sought because "we knew that's exactly what they were setting out to do."

Yet some authorities feel business has a real difficulty in steering a course between opposing legal doctrines. "This conflict is between the hard competition of the Sherman Antitrust Act and the soft competition of the Robinson-Patman Act," said Paul J. Winschel, trust lawyer for the Pittsburgh firm of Reed, Smith, Shaw & McClay.

"Hard competition," says Winschel, "means you go into the marketplace and use every reasonably fair tactic to secure as large a portion of the market as you can. Selective price discrimination is a very appropriate method of doing

107

this. Price-cutting is the very best evidence of the hard type of competition. Soft competition in the Robinson-Patman Act dictates you can't arbitrarily discriminate in price between various competing customers. The tendency of the act is to promote pricing uniformity and pricing rigidity."

In complying with the Sherman Act, says Winschel, a company is playing "Russian roulette" with the Robinson-Patman Act. In banning price discrimination and predatory pricing, the aim of the law is to protect the little guy against the big guy. There is some inhibition even for an industry as dedicated to price uniformity as steel. A company like U. S. Steel must be careful about offering research assistance to one customer if it is not prepared to do the same thing for the whole market. A big company may meet import competition on a selective basis but had better be prepared to document the competition.

More important than technicalities, though, is the knowledge that a big company had better not grow at the expense of the smaller companies. If a price war broke out in steel, the big mills would be hurt but they would survive. Others might not.

Most of the steel collusion cases followed the same pattern. The mills issued denials. They entered "not guilty" pleas at first. The pleas were eventually changed to "no contest." In dealing with pleas and sentences, judges have dwelt on the seriousness of price-fixing. In the castings case, Judge Sylvester J. Ryan said the industry had a blind spot on antitrust matters. In the sheet cases, this warning came from Judge Edward Weinfeld: "People have the mistaken idea that an antitrust violation is a technical infraction, a white-collar offense with no moral taint involved. There is nothing respectable in such a violation."

Yet the government fixes prices in wartime. State milk commissions will jump on a supplier who cuts prices. The act of price regulation is not inherently immoral. The law recognizes that some types of regulation are beneficial. Price collusion is wrong, of course, but it's not like robbing a bank.

The sheet indictment was to remain a quiet concern of steel men over the next 1½ years. In early 1964, it seemed to be the only worry.

The market continued to behave beautifully. The civilized state of labor relations was brought out again by reports from Kaiser Steel. "Workers are actually picking up nails which fall to the floor," said Edgar Kaiser. He was talking about the cooperative spirit produced by the sharing plan started in 1963. During the first 10 months the plan was in effect, Kaiser had reduced labor and material costs by more than $9 million. Workers received $3 million under the new plan for an average of 46¢ an hour.

The company had gone from a deficit of $5 million in 1962 to a profit of $11 million in 1963. There were various factors at work, but it was thought that the attitude of employees was of key importance. Since the plan started, Kaiser had gotten 690 cost-cutting ideas from workers. Most had been solid, constructive suggestions. "More than 9 out of 10 submitted at Fontana have been put into effect," said Edgar Kaiser.

Marvin Miller of the union said this record proved that steelworkers have good ideas "when given the opportunity." "Efficiency and security are two sides of the same coin," said Miller. "The most surprising thing to me is the suggestions that have come in," said Dr. George Taylor, public member of the long-range committee. The only doubtful comments came from G. E. Balsley, vice-president of labor relations for Kaiser. There had been suggestions, he conceded, but most of them involved materials. Very few dealt with reductions in labor costs.

Marvin Miller attributed this pattern to the fact that a

fresh field had been opened up. "While labor savings are an old story, the material incentive is a new thing." Balsley was not so sure. One of the reasons Kaiser had adopted the plan was to get away from past practice restrictions in things like crew assignment. It had been thought that with assured worker security, management would gain the right to make job changes freely. That hadn't happened. "The employment security thought in the plan isn't getting through to the men," said Balsley. "We know that we have found some problems in not being able to identify the man who has been displaced technologically. Because of the operation of the seniority program, we lose him immediately.

One of the key objectives has been to guarantee a man against job loss due to new technology. The theory was that the normal attrition rate was high enough to offset productivity gains if machinery could be devised to carry men through the transition period. One of the difficulties was that the first big technical change came at the time of a market slump. As a result, there was confusion about who was being protected from what. "We haven't got the union's agreement to let us unilaterally cut crew sizes," said Balsley. There were bugs in the new plan but both sides were working of them. The overall initial results seemed tremendously hopeful.

In the marketplace, prices seemed to reflect the nice balance of supply and demand. On April 9, the price of 302 and 304 stainless strip was cut 7¢ a pound, wiping out entirely the differential between these grades and lower nickel types. When the price gap had gotten too big, various mills had come up with special grades. Some of these were suspected of being low-price versions of expensive steels. The proliferation was creating confusion and distortion.

Eventually, Republic Steel cut through the whole confusion by reducing the 302 and 304 grades. This meant the same price was being charged for 201, which had a minimum of 3.5 per cent nickel; for 301, which had a 6 per cent minimum; and for 302, which had at least 8 per cent nickel. In seeking a price level that would bring demand up to supply, stainless producers had pretty well forgotten about costs.

On April 13, Kaiser Steel cut the price of linepipe, saying this was a move to meet informal cutting. On May 6, U. S. Steel eliminated the regional premium on rod and wire at seaboard plants. Other products were adjusted downward at points hit by imports. Earlier, U. S. Steel had made its strongest move against foreign steel by coming out with a common quality rod and wire priced $20 a ton under the standard quality.

The jockeying in stainless continued. In April, U. S. Steel increased the jobber discount on sheet and plate to 10 per cent. On June 3, Allegheny Ludlum came back with reduction of 5 per cent to direct users. Technically, the jobber allowance remained 10 per cent but only half of this could be kept.

Although prices were reduced on certain products, there were also price increases. On April 20, Jones & Laughlin boosted conduit prices. On June 9, Pittsburgh Steel tightened the quantity extras on mechanical tubing. "The pricing was such that people were buying as little as possible at a time," said Robert E. Lauterbach, sales vice-president of Pittsburgh Steel. "We don't want to be in the warehouse business."

Base prices of plate, sheet, bar, and structural were firm. There was some playing with extras but nothing that was considered important. "You're talking about the chaff," said a sales executive. That was the setting as the summer of 1964 approached. Business was good but not overpowering.

In the summer of 1964, things started to go wrong. The first difficulty was that the mills guessed wrong about demand. "We forecast in our annual report that the steel industry would produce 110 million tons of ingots," said Charles Beeghly, Jones & Laughlin chairman. "We now regard this as a conservative estimate. An additional 2 or 3 million tons of ingots is realizable."

That was in April. By July, Beeghly was saying ingot output would equal or top the record of 117 million tons of 1955. At this same time, steel men were starting to say privately that production could even get up to 120 million tons. Actual production in 1964 was 127 million tons. After 5 flat years, the mills just couldn't believe business was as good as it seemed. Plans were made on the basis of a summer letdown. Maintenance shutdowns were scheduled for the warm months. Vacations were allowed to bunch up in this period.

There was no real letdown. Shipments dropped from 7 million tons in June to about 6.9 million tons in July. In August, shipments were back up to nearly 7 million tons. After a long period when shipments had averaged around 6 million tons a month, it took some hustling to get out 7 million tons. Vacations and deferred maintenance disrupted production. The mills fell a little behind on orders. The lag wasn't much; deliveries stretched out 2 or 3 weeks, but it was enough to alert purchasing agents. In late August, the auto companies decided they couldn't wait until January 1 to see if steel contracts would be reopened by the steel union.

No strike could be called until 120 days after the reopener but the auto people felt they had to begin lining up extra steel much sooner. At the close of August, they began outlining stockpiling programs to the mills. These called for putting in an extra 60 days' steel supply by the following April. Once word of the auto move got out, other users figured they had better start squirreling away steel. This inventory push was imposed on record consumption.

Use of steel rose in 1964 to about 85 million tons, up from an approximate 75 million tons in 1963.

The result was inevitable. By the end of September, mills were informally controlling distribution of plate, sheet, and bar. By December, shipments were over 7.6 million tons. Foreign producers moved in quickly to grab excess orders. Imports had been averaging about 500,000 tons a month since the 1963 negotiations. In November, they jumped to 700,000 tons. There was a dip during the dock strike but foreign deliveries zoomed over 1 million tons in March of 1965.

So one phase of the steel labor programs had already failed by the summer of 1964. An old-fashioned inventory boom had begun. That was unfortunate but not necessarily critical. If the mills could get a settlement by January 1, they could head off the worst part of the buildup.

But now the steel jinx really started working. At his quarterly press conference in July, Roger Blough talked about prices. Prices, he said, "certainly weren't at the level they should be." U. S. Steel wasn't contemplating increases "at the moment" but "if demand for steel should continue strong and the supply should get tighter, I would hope to see some firming. . . ."

According to one knowledgeable steel man, this exposition was strictly an impromptu reflex. Asked about prices, Blough had said, sure, it would be nice to have increases. Others insist Roger Blough never in his life has spoken without considering the meaning of every syllable. In any case, his remarks that day got a pretty good play in the papers. President Johnson warned that steel price increases would conflict with national interest (Aug. 8).

On July 30, Edmund F. Martin, now chairman of Bethlehem, had his quarterly say. "We aren't satisfied with our earnings, not by any means. In view of our costs and capital commitments, we are constantly looking at the price

113

situation." Asked about what President Johnson might say, Martin gave a spirited reply. "I'm not worried about anything in Washington on price increases."

On September 30, Joseph Block of Inland Steel discussed steel profits. "The clear fact is that we do not make a satisfactory return on the vast sums of money invested in the industry. A week later in Chicago, Roger Blough said the steel return on sales was down 13 per cent from the '47–'49 period. He noted pointedly that both political parties were supporting the notion of business freedom.

In mid-October, Logan T. Johnston of Armco Steel said increases were "needed now" on more than half his company's products. On October 20, Bethlehem Steel increased prices on large linepipe $5 a ton. U. S. Steel followed on October 25, saying the net increase came to 1 per cent. On October 28, President Johnson let it be known that he was keeping close tabs on steel prices. This was one of those stories that did not directly quote the President but supposedly had the official stamp of approval.

U. S. Steel's stock dropped $2 that day. Bethlehem's Martin had an inspired thought when he faced reporters also the same day. "I know what's uppermost in your minds but pardon me if I don't answer any questions on prices." It was now too late, however. President Johnson had already committed himself to opposing a price increase. The mills would go into negotiations with their escape hatch closed. It probably didn't make the slightest bit of difference but the long series of price comments made it doubly sure the President would not overlook wage-price doings in steel.

While the price issue was being joined, real problems were building up on the opposite flank. On September 9, Chrysler Corporation reached a labor agreement with the United Autoworkers of America. Among other things, the agreement called for early retirement pensions for men

114

with 30 years of service. A man qualifying could collect as much as $400 a month. In addition, the normal pension rates were nearly doubled. There was never any official cost put on the package but it was generally estimated as having a value of at least 55¢, or 4.8 per cent a year. It clearly exceeded the government's 3.2 per cent guideline.

President Johnson argued that the auto terms could not be taken as a general precedent. "Both labor and management realize the unique nature of the auto labor settlement. I expect that other industries, with profits below the high levels in autos, will not use the auto settlement as a pattern." The guideline, he said, continued to present a sound standard for "noninflationary wage and price decisions." To steel management this meant: (1) the government was not abandoning its surveillance, and (2) no matter how high a settlement you made, the government would find a way to call it noninflationary.

There was one other disquieting note in the auto situation. The union struck General Motors Corp. and the strike lasted 31 days, long after economic terms had been negotiated with the UAW leadership. Something similar happened at Ford. It was not unusual for the auto industry to have local strikes under these circumstances. Even during the contract term, locals may legally strike on certain plant matters. Unlike the steel contract, the auto agreements leave wide areas in which management can make decisions without appeal to outside arbitration, but the union is free to strike against these decisions.

Apart from this, the Autoworker leadership supposedly encourages locals to let off a little steam at negotiating time. There seemed to be a little extra steam in the auto strikes, and they were to be recalled vividly by steel people in subsequent negotiations. At the time, though, the big thing seemed to be the size of the auto package. The immediate thought was that the Steelworkers would try and match or top the auto terms. There were fears that the moderation of 1962 and 1963 would go down the drain.

"My hunch," said one company bargainer, "is that the auto settlement will give us a problem beyond the capabilities of the Human Relations Committee." Another company man was less certain. "The only thing we can say is that knotty problems have been solved in the past. There is nothing more difficult than in the past. I think we are better prepared now." However, both men made it clear that nothing much had happened yet in the Human Relations talks. "The issues have not yet been sharply defined," said one. Very much later people were saying there would have been a quick, quiet settlement if events had followed the normal course. This was considered far from certain in September of 1964.

1964 · THE BOMB

The Steelworkers convention, which began in Atlantic City on September 21, gave no hint of special trouble. Dave McDonald unfurled a dramatic new concept—total job security. "We must end," said the union, "this idea that a Steelworker is a Steelworker only when the employer says he needs him, by the hour, by the week, by the month or even by the year. The inhumanity of layoffs must cease." "All we're asking," said another union official, "is that the companies give workers the same consideration they give machines. A company will try and get full utilization of a tool. It will set aside a certain amount of money as the tool is expended."

This sounded like a pretty formidable plan. "It's socialism, pure and simple," said A. S. Glossbrenner, president of Youngstown Sheet & Tube. Another steel official noted that full employment obligations had gotten foreign steel mills in trouble. "They have to pay people so they do the logical thing and put them to work regardless of domestic demand."

Yet the union proposals did suggest another accommoda-

117

tion might be in the works. McDonald had devised a notion that was enormously attractive to the workers. Despite improved business, job security was still a prime concern of men in the mills. On the other hand, the companies were already committed to a considerable amount of security. With Supplemental Unemployment Benefits (SUB), workers who were laid off got two-thirds of their take-home pay for a full year. There were pension, vacation, sickness, and disability funds.

By consolidating the money already available and adding a little, it was possible the companies could go a long way toward fulfilling the new need without excessive cost. The union was seeking to expand existing plans by giving full income protection and by giving lifetime protection. Union officials explained that this might be done initially by giving unlimited SUB to a limited number of senior workers. The whole approach suggested the Steelworkers were concentrating on solutions rather than price tags.

Dave McDonald insisted he was not out to top or duplicate the Autoworker settlement. "They have their problems; we have ours." He also had some encouraging words on the Human Relations meetings. "We haven't run out of problems but we're having more meetings than the last time. I'd say we're further ahead than at this stage last time."

There was one rumble at the convention. Various resolutions were introduced calling for compulsory retirement of union officers. If adopted, some of these would have retired Dave McDonald on the spot. The resolution finally adopted established 68 as the retirement age, but said top officers could run for office if they were below 68 when their term started. This assured McDonald of another two terms.

There didn't seem to be any real steam behind the move to ease McDonald out. One of those who favored forced retirement at 60 was Donald Rarick, a rank-and-filer

118

who made a surprisingly strong bid for the presidency in 1956 but who was not able to get serious support since. The top organization seemed strongly united behind McDonald. One of those who spoke against the ouster move was Joseph Germano, director of the big Chicago district and one of the powers within the union. "When [his people] decide to change directors or change International officers, they know how to go about it within the Constitution of the United Steelworkers of America. They don't have to circulate resolutions for compulsory retirement unless they believe in it."

This was possibly a little ambiguous but there seemed to be nothing equivocal about other Germano comments. McDonald was "my very good friend." "I love Dave McDonald." Some of the expressions of friendship were in the past tense. In the retirement statement, there was possibly a hint that other means besides retirement would be used to get rid of an officer. But you had to be looking awfully hard to see dissention in these inflections. Not many were looking that hard. General feeling was that if there had been a challenge, Dave McDonald had beaten it down and was still firmly in the saddle. As secretary of the resolutions committee, director Joseph Molony read a resolution that considered it "a matter of great good fortune that David J. McDonald is president of United Steelworkers of America."

Nevertheless, rumors persisted. In late October, district director William Hart let it slip that one of the biggest labor stories in history would be breaking the next week. He said the whole labor movement was in a restless state. He noted that the Autoworkers were having trouble getting men back to work after a big settlement. "We have a meeting in my district tonight," said Hart. "I have no idea what I'm going to be walking into." Having given this tantalizing hint, he clammed up. It looked as though something important was brewing within the Steelworkers. The headlines started to form: "Trouble in Paradise." But then the headline faded as a check of other sources turned up only the usual grumbling of an election year. "We have a few problems politically within our organization which I think are rather silly," said Howard Hague, USWA vice-president.

District director Hugh Carcella referred to "splinter groups who are never satisfied." "They have no issue," said another union source. Hague was asked about the complaint that district and union officials were not being kept informed. "They just don't read their mail," he said. Emphatically, he stated, there was no special problem.

Then on November 5, the dream of stable labor relations in steel got its final kick in the teeth. I. W. Abel, secretary-treasurer, announced he would oppose David J. McDonald in Steelworkers presidential elections the following February. It was quickly apparent that Abel had strong backing within the organization. Running with him was Joe Molony, director of the Buffalo district and the man who bucked McDonald's candidate—Hague—in the 1955 vice-presidential race. Walter J. Burke, Milwaukee director, was running for secretary-treasurer. On November 12, Joe Germon of Chicago announced "wholehearted support" for Abel. William Mahoney, national director for Canada, said he was backing Abel.

The dissident group had gotten the jump in lining up key men and territories. "Our decision to run is predicated on indications of strong support," said Abel. Attempts were made to gloss over the disruption of bargaining that would result from the political fight. "I am elected president until June," said McDonald. "I certainly think we'll have an agreement by then." "It certainly should not have any bearing on the conduct of negotiations," said Abel. "We're not going to interfere with that at all."

The companies went along with this charade. On November 12, they joined with the union in a reassuring statement. "We intend to solve our problems cooperatively and in timely fashion." Human Relations talks were being stepped up. December meetings of company-union bargaining teams were scheduled. "It is our determination to cooperate to solve by agreement such problems as may come before the parties in collective bargaining without the need or desire on either side to precipitate a crisis on May 1, 1965." The release referred to the successful experience of 1962 and 1963 and said there was a "solid basis" for expecting a quick, quiet settlement.

There was just one trouble with this statement. It had been drawn up before the union's political fight started. Privately, the companies were sick. There could be no bargaining, they said, until the political contest had been settled and people knew who was running the Steelworkers. The election wasn't until February 9, 3 months before a possible strike deadline.

The Abel line of attack centered on the centralized power of McDonald and his staff. "The rank and file want more voice in negotiations," said Walter Burke. Joe Molony promised that "every local member will have his chance with his local boss to try and straighten out local conditions." A resolution passed by a District 31 conference said the union should be prepared to strike on local issues and "no contract (should) be signed until these issues are settled."

At the beginning of its official campaign on December 20, the Abel group issued this manifesto: "The basic democratic traditions of our union have been subverted over a number of years. To an even greater degree the decision-making process has been concentrated at the top. Our constitution gives the members the right to regain control of their union by electing officials responsive to their needs and desires. We intend to restore rank-and-file control over

121

basic policies. We intend to restore the bargaining table to its rightful position as the proper place for collective bargaining. We intend to return the Human Relations Committee to its original function—that of fact-finding—and discontinue its encroachment on policy-making functions."

Neglect of local problems had resulted in a "disgraceful backlog of unresolved grievances. . . . We present the rank and file with a clear-cut choice between conscientious trusteeship . . . and the so-called 'mutual trusteeship,' in which the union presumed to solve its problems while also serving management."

In later statements, the Abel group charged McDonald with "private, personal negotiations with individuals whom he regards as his social equals. . . ." McDonald's rule was tagged as "tuxedo leadership." McDonald was pictured as a high-living dude who had grown remote from the membership and gotten too cozy with management.

Control of negotiations had been monopolized by the President and his staff people. The Human Relations privacy had denied the rank and file any say in talks and any information on what was happening. One result of all this had been inferior settlements. Another had been neglect of local problems. The "summit" approach of McDonald and his technicians had shut elected officers out of bargaining.

The Abel thrust coincided with what seemed to be a general wave of worker unrest. In the International Union of Electrical Workers, James B. Carey faced his first formal opposition since the union was founded in 1949. Paul Jenning had been nominated to run against Carey in the November 9 convention of the IUE. W. A. "Tony" Boyle of the Mineworkers faced a challenge by Steve Kochis, a rank-and-filer from Pennsylvania. This was the Mineworker's first presidential fight since the 1920's. In the Autoworkers, there had been local strikes after the general agreements. Now, the Steelworkers were having their first serious fight.

"I think there is unrest in labor," said Abel considerably later. "There is fear and insecurity, particularly in industrial work, where a revolution is taking place. Look at this new plant of Bethlehem in the Midwest—10,000 workers will be able to turn out 10 per cent of the nation's output. Steelworkers have spent lifetimes developing skills. Now they see where a couple of oxygen furnaces take the place of a battery of open hearths. In the final analysis, this is the thing that has produced unrest and insecurity. The only place the workers have to turn is their unions. In some cases, they have become disillusioned with the union's leadership."

There was no question the Abel tacticians had hit a responsive chord when they promised to right the wrongs of the little guys. The force of the response was to influence negotiations for the next 12 months. In the opinion of management people, however, the opposition did not spring spontaneously from the yearnings of the masses. R. Conrad Cooper afterwards called it a "palace guard revolt."

One company bargainer put it this way: "The muscle had been taken away from the locals." It was not a move by the workers to throw out the bosses; it was an organization split. If anything, the organization was asserting its power over a usurper. This was evident when nominations for the election were tabulated. Abel was seconded by more than 1300 locals against something like 900 for McDonald. In Canada, Abel had an edge of more than two to one.

McDonald called these returns "interesting but insignificant. . . . The results only demonstrated that participation by members was extremely low." At the nominating meeting of Inland Steel's 18,000-man local, less than 170 turned out to vote. In other locations, similar ratios were reported. It remained to be seen if the organization could deliver the

123

vote but it was clear enough that Abel controlled the organization. By a slim but firm margin, he had district backing to swing the union's executive board his way.

The curious fact was that McDonald, the incumbent, was the outsider, whereas the rebel faction represented the established order. On the matter of issues, the normal positions were also reversed. The new group was pushing for the old ways of doing business. The incumbent was the advocate of new ways.

Having been taken by surprise in the push, McDonald could never gain the initiative. He was automatically on the defensive on issues. He could never quite match the aggressive tone of his opponents. He had a strong case. During his time as president, the basic steel rate had gone from $1.43 an hour to $2.28 an hour. Pension, insurance, and holiday benefits had been improved. Shift and holiday premiums had been improved. SUB and extended vacation programs had been negotiated. As the companies later pointed out, the pay of the Steelworkers had risen to 88¢ an hour more than the average of all manufacturing.

However, McDonald was never able to focus attention on this record. The big issue was his style of leadership. This involved his personality, his manner of living, his relations with locals, and his method of conducting bargaining. "Hogwash," he said to charges that he had lost touch with the rank and file. "I've shaken more hands and seen more people than anybody in this union. I spent only 30 days at home last year." His supporters argued that his place in Palm Springs was no more palatial than Abel's summer home in Deep Creek, Maryland.

The Abel people charged that McDonald spent his time hobnobbing with the jet set. McDonald men answered that Phil Murray had always insisted union officials wear ties and travel first class. "How much can you spend?" asked one close associate of the Steelworkers chief. "You go into

124

a town. You can only eat one steak dinner. I've been with Dave. He has worked 18 hours for the union." At the root of all this talk was the fundamental charge that McDonald liked management people. He wanted to be liked and accepted by them. With his golf club and his Palm Springs home and his nightclubbing, he had turned his back on his class.

McDonald would protest mightily against this. "I was born in the shadow of the steel stacks and this is the only life I have ever known or ever hope to know." But McDonald was not a mill worker. He no more reflected the roughness of the open-hearth shop than Ben Fairless bore any traces of his upbringing as a miner's son in Pigeon Run, Ohio. McDonald looked like the chief executive of a million-man organization. That is not the way a labor leader is supposed to look. To some people, in management as well as labor, his genteel ways were uppity.

"When I go to New York, I like to stop at Twenty-One," said one middle manager. "Who do you think I saw the last time? Dave McDonald. It kinda got me." It didn't matter that McDonald had 50 times more responsibility; this individual resented seeing a labor leader mingling with the swells. McDonald seemed deeply conscious of the social situation. In his speech and manner, he seemed to go overboard in trying to show labor leaders were not roughnecks. At New York sound-off sessions, he described how one official wanted to cover all problems at once. "But I told him—wait a minute—let's go about this *ad seriatum.*"

McDonald was given to effusive displays that rubbed some people wrong. "I am a candidate for president of the United Steelworkers of America not for personal pride but because I love you." McDonald took office in 1953 just in time for the good will tour with Ben Fairless. It was noted by Vin Sweeney that this fraternization with the bosses did not sit well with all steelworkers. "Some of

125

them were too stuck in the old-fashioned, table-pounding, breast-beating ways of labor unions in days gone by," wrote Sweeney.

At the 1954 Steelworkers convention, McDonald may have ruffled a few more feathers. "The days of Andrew Carnegie and people like him are gone," he announced. "Hundreds of thousands of stockholders own the great corporations of America. . . . These stockholders . . . employ a group of managers. These managers are simply employees of those corporations. Then there is another group of employees known as the working force. Both of these groups have this mutual trusteeship. . . . Both, of course, have an obligation to the owner."

This may have been strong stuff for veterans of the barricades. There may have been more resentment when McDonald extended his goodwill tour by visiting plants of Jones & Laughlin with Admiral Ben Moreell, J & L chairman. It should be noted that the call for brotherhood was followed by a 1-day strike in 1955, a 1-month strike in 1956, and a 116-day strike in 1959. The peaceful interlude ended when the 1955 boom started. The Human Relations harmony might very well have been swept away by the 1965 boom. McDonald did like nice people, but he was not dumb and he was not blind to the realities of union politics. Once he tried to recruit a Princeton graduate for the Steelworkers. What would happen, asked the prospect, if you left. "They'd tear you to pieces in 10 minutes," McDonald supposedly replied.

Without any prompting, he might have decided that 1965 was not the year to display friendly feelings toward management. And the essence of the Human Relations spirit was cooperation if not friendship. The idea was to approach problems in an objective manner, not trying to gain a victory but only to find fair solutions. ". . . it has come to be recognized by both sides that equity and understanding must play a greater part in labor relations," said Heath Larry after the 1963 talks. This recognition might have gone down the drain in any event. With the election fight, it was automatically doomed. And with fraternization a specific issue, it was doubly dead.

Also discarded was the Human Relations tendency toward scientific determination of wage and benefit matters. The idea was that if you got enough information and studied it hard enough, the right answers would be apparent to all. Ultimately, the analysis might be fully mechanized. At Kaiser, there was a formula for measuring progress. There was another formula for dividing up the fruits of progress. In moving to make bargaining a science, the Human Relations program tended to elevate technical specialists. Or maybe it was the other way around. Maybe bargaining became more technical because technical people were given key roles.

At any rate, staff people did become more important. Marvin Miller was the driving force behind the Kaiser plan and other complex programs. Ben Fisher was the arbitration expert. John Tomayko was the insurance and pension specialist. Miller was possibly the key figure in this picture. A slim, soft-spoken man, he had the imagination, brainpower, and competence to formulate workable systems in the most tangled areas of job security.

Miller was union coordinator of the Human Relations Committee. He was the man McDonald turned to when a detailed question came up at press conferences. More than any other, perhaps, he represented the technical spirit that had developed at the top of the Steelworkers. Again, this spirit might well have been washed away in any event. The Abel revolt had been pictured as a revolt against intellectualism—as a move to substitute brawn for brains.

Actually, the staff people were dedicated unionists. No one chafed more than Marvin Miller at the failure of the union to make tougher stands. No one was more impatient with the slowness of the Human Relations procedure. When the 1963 talks were dragging to an end, he predicted the Human Relations format would either be discarded the next time or radically revised. Free exploration was all right up to a point, he said, but you had to start nailing things down.

If there were already doubts that steel bargaining could be reduced to a science, the political fight changed these doubts to certainty. The Abel people attacked the extension of fact-finding to bargaining. They called for demotion of technical fact-finders. One final issue was related to all bargaining but particularly to the Human Relations type of bargaining. McDonald did represent strong, centralized leadership. He never dominated his union in the iron-handed manner of a John L. Lewis, but he did stand out as the leader—as the one man who could speak for a million men.

This kind of leadership was vital to the Human Relations approach. In the coal industry, the top labor and management people would meet on a continuing or intermittent basis. There would be no set time for working out new terms. Since the early 1950's coal contracts had never been formally reopened. The steel people were working toward informality and flexibilty. For calm, cooperative consideration of problems, they said, you had to get away from rigid contract spans and final strike deadlines. You had to get away from the "crisis" atmosphere.

In theory, this approach did not limit participation. Company people argued that there had probably been broader treatment of problems in the Human Relations days than in the period when the pattern was negotiated with U. S. Steel and then applied to other mills. But centralized authority was required. If the program was not to be an academic study, there had to be someone who had power to make commitments without a lot of official ratification. It was this power the Abel people specifically attacked. The wage-policy committee had had "virtually no chance to participate in . . . negotiations." McDonald had made agreements in "private huddles with the industry." He had specialized in "summit" bargaining. What Abel wanted was a return to official, formal, arms-length bargaining. His big pitch was that there should be broad participation and strict limits on the authority of top bargainers. "I don't feel I have all the wisdom in the world as to what's good for the Steelworkers," Abel said later. "It might take a little longer but the democratic process works best in the long run."

This was the key question in subsequent bargaining. Some company people contended it was impossible to have any negotiations unless the union leadership assumed full responsibility. "You can't run collective bargaining like a referendum," said one company man. "Why not?" demanded Joe Molony, Abel's running mate. When people talked about a disciplined union, said Molony, they meant one where you could take the leader over to the Duquesne Club and make a quick deal with him.

In any case, the Human Relations period was over. The one great puzzle was the man who led the attack against it. Iorwith W. Abel seemed out of character as a rebel. Some accounts have it that the rebellion itself had been brewing since 1955, when Molony opposed McDonald's candidate, Howard Hague, for the Steelworkers vice-presidency. Others said the strong showing of Donald Rarick in his 1956 race against McDonald was due to lukewarm support of the union chief by district leaders.

According to one source, the final decision to depose McDonald did not come until after the retirement hassle at the convention. If McDonald had not bucked a reasonable retirement rule, said this source, he could have had another term without any fuss. When McDonald insisted on another 9 years, the dissidents decided to make an open fight. But again, I. W. Abel was an incongruous figure in this picture of dissent and discontent. A reserved but amiable man, Abel had always seemed the loyal subordinate, the inconspicuous plodder who might be found in the far background of settlement pictures. McDonald said he never had the slightest hint that "Abe" was nurturing grand ambitions. McDonald said he could never figure out what did cause the break.

Born in Magnolia, Ohio, of Welsh extraction, Abel started out as a foundry worker in Canton, Ohio. He took part in the early organizing efforts of the Steelworkers, became district director, and moved into the secretary-treasurer job in 1953 when McDonald succeeded Phil Murray as president. Abel is a compact man with sturdy, regular features. He has a deep voice that booms out from a platform. There is nothing rough or uncivilized about him, but he does have the weathered look of a man who might have worked with his hands once.

In every way, he is a contrast with McDonald. Where McDonald is emotional and dramatic, Abel is stoical and conversational. Abel is not above skirting a tough question; he is surprisingly quick-witted, but he tends to be more direct and candid than McDonald. McDonald has the ability to project and excite. With his white hair and lofty profile, he causes heads to turn when he walks through a hotel lobby. There is a buzz, a murmur. Abel looks like the guy next door. On television or in pictures, he has a flat, wooden appearance. Where McDonald expands with public exposure, Abel contracts a little. Like Conrad Cooper, Abel comes through with greater force when you get closer to him and see him in person.

If Abel did not seem the type to lead a revolt, he did fit in very well with the organizational structure he was advocating. His modesty and simplicity made his attacks on labor dictatorships ring true. He was not a man you would picture hogging the spotlight or asserting his will in an autocratic manner. In the opinion of some observers at the time, he didn't have the fire to start a rebellion. There was speculation that Abel was a figurehead, chosen by the directors to be the front man for the fight. The theory was that the directors would manipulate Abel or get rid of him once McDonald was out of the way. This theory was later to be deflated when the wishes of one of the most powerful directors were rejected by the union. Nevertheless, Abel has remained an enigmatic figure. There is a growing suspicion that his surface mildness conceals the inner toughness of a leader. Management people hope this is so. At some point, they say, Abel is going to have to say "No" to his constituents and make it stick.

On November 16, the union held its sound-off session in New York. Some 700 local presidents aired their gripes at the Roosevelt Hotel. Problems discussed included subcontracting work by foremen, incentive pay for maintenance workers, job scheduling, and grievance procedures. "I would say 95 per cent of the discussions centered on contract improvements," said Dave McDonald. "The great emphasis was on protection of jobs." He said the questions brought up were not really "local" conditions. Things like subcontracting had to be dealt with in national contracts. There were complaints about parking lots and washroom facilities but most of the beefs involved more general conditions. This was a distinction that was to plague negotiators in coming months and one that never did get straightened out to the satisfaction of all.

On November 28, President Lyndon Johnson touched on steel prices and wages. "Steel prices have been essentially stable since October 1963 and I hope and I expect they can remain that way." The President mentioned that steel profits were up 26 per cent. Steel employment had risen by 80,000 since last December. "As the period of bargaining approaches, I am anxious to preserve stability in this great industry. . . . I also look forward to a responsible settlement which preserves stable labor costs per unit and thus contributes to continued stability in steel prices. I am sure that the parties have the wisdom to reach a new agreement without a strike and without labor cost or price increases. . . ."

So there it was. The President had said again he wanted no price increase. He had indicated his personal interest in a peaceful settlement. At this early date, Mr. Johnson had committed himself to what management considered incompatible aims. At a time when the union was steamed up by its election fight, management was told to make a peaceful settlement with noninflationary terms. From then on, said some authorities, it was up to the Administration to decide which of its goals—peace or stability—should be sacrificed.

On December 3, the union's wage-policy committee released its bargaining program. This had something for everyone. Total job security was spelled out as meaning unlimited SUB for senior workers. There were various demands on crew sizes and other phases of plant practice. The policy statement called for a "substantial" wage increase. It called for higher pensions. There was also a demand that workers be allowed to retire on full pension regardless of age. There was no special emphasis on this benefit, which had been an important part of the auto settlement.

The union was fairly specific in its listing of demands. It got into such things as the accumulation of warning slips and the details of the grievance procedure. Some of the language was challenging. In some plants, management had been "abusing its power." Answers on grievances were being "dictated by the upper echelons of management." The mills were enjoying a "prosperity unparalleled in their history."

Finally, the policy document made official what had been considered certain earlier. It called for formal reopening of steel contracts January 1. This would permit a strike 120 days later.

The last prop of the Human Relations program—flexible contract span—was thus officially knocked away. The steel industry was heading into its first session of crisis bargaining since 1959. The final report of the Human Relations Committee was made a week or so later. There was some talk about useful studies and tentative recommendations. According to a union official, however, there were no agreements, tentative or otherwise. The companies, he later claimed, had missed their chance to avoid a lot of grief.

On December 14, on the eve of the bargaining start, the companies hit back at the wage-policy statement. Steel profits were not all that great; steel earnings were 88¢ over the industry average; labor costs had risen 33¢ since October of 1961. Job security, said the companies, could only be achieved by keeping down costs and helping the industry meet world competition. Imports had resulted in the loss of 35,000 jobs. The American share of the world steel market had shrunk from 46 per cent in 1950 to 26 per cent in 1963.

Finally, the companies said steel productivity had increased by only 2 per cent annually in the last 6 years, while steel employment costs had risen 5 per cent annually in this period. "The union's wage-policy program," said the companies, "goes either to taking for the Steelworkers an unfair share of the proceeds of the business at the expense of others or increasing restriction upon the companies. . . ."

The union was called on to reconsider its decision on a reopening notice "and not put the country to the disturbance of a potential crisis date." This was the strongest public blast to come from management since the 1959 talks. Nevertheless, R. Conrad Cooper said the two sides would continue to observe the Human Relations spirit of privacy. This seems a little inconsistent with his opening potshot, but he insisted the companies were simply responding to a public union document.

McDonald came back the next day and said "almost all the figures in the companies statement are incorrect or used erroneously." It wasn't a promising start. Even before actual bargaining, the two sides were bickering in the newspapers. But the talks did get underway December 15 without further incident. At these early sessions, large company-union delegations for each of the 11 mills met separately. There were more than 300 at the U. S. Steel meetings. Bethelehem and the others also had large groups. This sort of thing had been done in the past but it had always been a fairly perfunctory thing. After a few days of griping, most of the people would be sent home and small subcommittees would be formed to do the real bargaining.

There didn't seem to be anything particularly different about the new talks. At one session, the union officials complained about the lack of training programs. The company countered that it was having trouble getting some men to accept training for better jobs. The company pointed out it had a considerable number of men who were bidding down—that is, applying for lower jobs. "We didn't hear any more about training after that," said the chief bargainer. In another situation, there was a discussion of overtime. The company said it was willing to hire more people but that labor just wasn't available.

After a week or so of talking, a recess was called until after the holidays. This first attempt at bargaining had not been entirely discouraging. Even company people were saying it was a healthy thing to air problems. The political fight apparently hadn't intruded too much on negotiations.

134

However, bargainers were reminded soon enough that the political fight had not gone away. On December 19, Abel officially launched his campaign in Chicago. On December 21 came official word that Abel had won the nominating contest by about 1300 to 900. McDonald supporters released a poll that showed their man favored by 50 per cent of the workers.

Meanwhile the companies were starting to do more than talk about prices. On December 7, U. S. Steel announced a $5 to $10 increase for thin-wall linepipe. On December 11, the same mill boosted oil-country tubing and casing. These were fairly minor moves. Total linepipe tonnage was only 3 per cent of steel shipments, and oil-country goods came to only 2 per cent. On December 21, however, Inland Steel increased the price of galvanized sheet $6 a ton or 3 per cent. Galvanized shipments had amounted to nearly 4 million tons in 1964, or more than 5 per cent of all steel produced.

On December 28 the word out of Washington was that President Johnson hoped the steel companies would show restraint in the price moves. That same day, Robert V. Roosa, Treasury undersecretary, warned that an across-the-board price increase would bring demands for a matching wage increase. He said the recent steel increases had not been harmful by themselves but that inflation could result if scattered increases were allowed to "creep across the board." Dave McDonald said the price hikes put the industry in "an even better position to met the urgent needs of Steelworkers."

1965 · A PREPOSTEROUS ASSEMBLY

In 1965, steel bargainers faced the job of negotiating a contract in the middle of a union fight. In addition, they had the task of satisfying Lyndon Johnson. The result, according to R. Conrad Cooper, was a "monstrosity," a "menagerie," and a "preposterous assembly of proposals."

On January 18, Federal Judge Sylvester J. Ryan handed down fines totaling $85,000 in the price-fixing cases involving steel castings and wheels. On January 26, Roger Blough of U. S. Steel issued a paper on prices. "The fact is," he said, "there has been practically no change in the average price of steel during the past six years." The Bureau of Labor Statistics, he said, reported a steel price index of 102.3 per cent in November; that was the same as the 1958 figure.

"Widely publicized increases," said Blough, "were offset completely by numerous and little publicized price decreases. . . ." A number of stainless prices had been cut by $200 to $300 a ton in the last 6 years, he noted. His point was a good one; it is something of a puzzle why the mills never did publicize price cuts. Blough also noted that some of the recent increases had done nothing but restore profit margins. On galvanized, the $6-a-ton steel increases had been preceded by increases of $60 a ton in zinc prices since 1963. He spoke of steel's declining profit position but he talked mainly about prices. Among other things he gave a pretty good blueprint of future price strategy when he described the isolated increases, the offsetting decreases, and the special cost of justification of moves.

On January 28, President Johnson touched on steel prices in his economic message to Congress. The President revealed that he had asked his Council of Economic Advisers to make a "special, detailed analysis" of steel price-and-wage increases. He said he was keeping a close watch on this general area. "I count on the sense of public responsibility of our labor leaders and our industrial leaders to do their full part to protect and extend our price stability."

As part of the CEA report contained in the message, there was an estimate that steel productivity had increased 4 per cent a year since 1959. This was the second report to come from the government on the subject. Earlier the Bureau of Labor Statistics had reported a 2 per cent figure for the annual productivity gain from 1957 to 1963. On January 31, Gardner Ackley, CEA chairman, said the Administration was disturbed about steel price increases. However, he noted special circumstances. "In several cases, they were merely restoring price cuts. . . ."

On February 4, President Johnson revealed that the study of steel prices and wages was going forward. Information had been received "from a good many of the companies." That same day, there was a warning from Ackley that the national outlook was good "if the Steelworkers did not get more than a 3.2 per cent wage boost." This was the third government guide to be used in the space of a few months. Dave McDonald shot back that the Administration had overlooked "15 other items" that would affect terms. Cost of living increases and job security needs were among the many other considerations.

On February 4, R. Conrad Cooper and the other top company bargainers gave a background briefing session for the press. They revealed that 2 per cent was about the limit of any offer they would voluntarily make. This information, they said, had been given the union early in talks. This unusual step had been taken to discourage any grand promises by the union's political candidates. Conrad Cooper said he felt the move had had its intended effect. "Both candidates have kept their heads down pretty well."

There were, however, obvious disadvantages to the maneuver. There was the danger that the union would treat the number as a starting position. The companies argued that they were not making an offer—that the actual settlement should be much less than 2 per cent. Nevertheless, they clearly put a floor under the settlement costs. The other big difficulty was that the companies were in a static position from then on. They had started with 2 per cent and they were determined to end with 2 per cent. This smacked of GE's "Boulwareism"—you made your best offer initially and refused to go through a lot of horsetrading. Unions considered this a refusal to bargain.

The companies could have gotten away from this snare by starting, as they had in recent years, with an offer of nothing. However, they could hardly have expected anyone to take this seriously in a year when the Autoworkers were getting 4.8 per cent or some such amount. The 2 per cent figure did have official government backing. It had been indicated by the Bureau of Labor Statistics (BLS)—the official agency for productivity. According to the companies, it took quite a bit of prodding to get the steel figure out of the government.

It was clear from the special study now being made that

the Administration wasn't particularly happy with Bureau of Labor Statistics reckoning. The following year, when Ewan Clague stepped out as chief of the bureau, the new commissioner announced that in the future there would be more "interpretation" of statistics. The sequence at this stage went like this. BLS had come out with 2 per cent. The Economic Council had mentioned 4 per cent and later 3.2 per cent. The companies had taken a stand of 2 per cent. The union was later to come out with demands management priced at 4 per cent. The CEA was to produce a special 3.0 per cent figure and then go back to 3.2 per cent.

Steel talks were resumed January 5, but now the union's political fight was very much in evidence. Top USWA officials spent a good part of their time maneuvering for position in the upcoming fight. McDonald had proposed that the American Arbitration Assn. be retained to oversee the election. He cited in this connection the court fight that had arisen in the International Union of Electrical Workers. There, Paul Jennings was charging fraud and seeking government intervention. McDonald's argument was that the Steelworkers would be damaged if the election did not return a clear-cut winner. It was also pointed out that Abel, as secretary-treasurer, controlled certain parts of the voting machinery. Ballots were sent out from his office. The final count came under his general supervision.

The Abel forces opposed the proposal, saying it "clearly violated both the USWA constitution and the Landrum-Griffin Act." They maintained the cost of outside monitoring would be prohibitive, that it was a slur on the honesty of the union, and that adequate safeguards were provided by having an outside group—the Honest Ballot Assn.— do the counting. Abel people asked why McDonald had not wanted neutral help when he was opposed by Don Rarick in 1957. This was a telling point, although Mc-

139

Donald said the cases were different—that the secretary-treasurer had been a disinterested party in 1957.

The voting on the monitoring was on a representation basis—each director got one vote for every 1000 members. The International officers—McDonald, Hague, and Abel —received a voting bloc based on the largest district. The Canadian director got a similar allotment in his territory. It worked out that the Abel forces got 741 votes to 641 for McDonald. This showed again that Abel had strong organizational support. It meant that the President of the union did not control his executive board. He could be thwarted in political moves. And as the Abel people pointed out, he was not in a position to make bargaining commitments for the union.

The Abel margin of control was demonstrated again in a vote against recognizing a newly formed union of some 600 USWA staff employees. The staff people had banded together to keep from being whipsawed by the political fight. McDonald had quickly offered recognition but the Abel people upset this decision on the grounds that a second organizing group should be considered. This was important only in that it demonstrated the solidarity of the Abel faction. The original staff group was ultimately recognized when a card check showed they had the required number of supporters.

The executive board votes pointed to a very close election. With the possibility of fraud already mentioned, there seemed a good chance that a thin voting margin would find the loser challenging results. While the union bickered internally, the companies were more or less standing by, tapping their feet. Finally on January 8, it was decided to recess the talks until after the February 9 election. The deterioration of bargaining relations showed up in the confused, quarrelsome manner in which talks were suspended.

On the previous day, said McDonald, Cooper had renewed his extension request and was turned down by the union. Then, continued McDonald, Cooper proposed a recess, saying the union "cannot conduct major bargaining in its present disturbed form." The companies' answer, even on local issues, would be "No" until the election was over. Thereupon a recess was agreed to. In the meantime, Abel was telling a press conference that he thought a press conference "might be in the best interest of all concerned."

The next day R. Conrad Cooper reported that the companies thought there should be an extension but that they were willing to bargain at once if the union would not grant an extra 120 days. At this point, it was perfectly obvious to everyone that there could be no serious bargaining. The fuss over the breakoff indicated that the two sides had reverted to a state in which nothing could be done without wrangling.

In any case, the talks were suspended and serious politicking began. On January 12, McDonald announced he had negotiated a tentative agreement with Alan Wood Steel Co. near Philadelphia. Described as a "major breakthrough" for total job security, the new plan provided jobless pay of unlimited duration for senior men. The amount of SUB was increased to 85 per cent of normal wages. In addition workers were guaranteed 95 per cent of their average pay in preceding quarters. They were assured 38 hours of work in any week they were on the job. There was a labor pool similar to that of Kaiser Steel, and there was some type of sharing arrangement. "It indicates," said McDonald, "that total job security can be done in basic steel. The idea of job security is not an ephemeral thing but a fact." The Abel people sneered at the new agreement. "You can't buy Utopia for 2¢," said Abel. A cost of 2¢ to 7¢ had been placed on the Alan Wood program.

In Chicago on January 14, the USWA wage-policy

committee officially turned down the company extension request. In reporting on negotiations, it said there had been "little concrete progress." There had been no sign of "willingness to solve the problems or meet the needs of the membership." R. Conrad Cooper charged the union with the responsibility for causing the crisis. The companies had bargained for a 120-day reopener and the union's election was taking away more than a month of this time. In refusing to establish a new 120-day period, said Cooper, the Steelworkers were setting the stage for a full, high-pressure crisis.

The union wasn't really listening. By now, both sides were too busy attacking each other to have much time for Cooper. Both factions had hired professional public relations men to grind out copy. At Gadsden, Alabama, Abel told listeners, the union "was tired of having the contracts negotiated in plush suites and business clubs." At Fairfield, Alabama, McDonald said Abel wanted to go back to the good old days. A certain amount of personal stuff did creep in. Abel was a racist. McDonald was a racist. McDonald was showing scare films of the Chicago massacre. Abel knew this wasn't true.

One new issue unexpectedly rang a bell. The Abel faction charged that McDonald had negotiated "inferior settlements in 1962 and 1963." Local conditions were getting worse; steel pay was lagging. "We simply haven't been getting our share of the benefits of increased productivity," said Abel. All this suggested a tougher, more militant brand of unionism. This point was picked up by a few publications. The *Wall Street Journal* quoted Abel as saying there were "worse things than a strike." (Abel did not deny the statement but said he had no recollection of making it to the *Journal*.)

Tom Campbell of *Iron Age* came out flatly and said Abel's election would increase the chances of a strike. This

142

statement on television and in print went to what some considered the nub of the matter. "The big issue," said a union official, "is who is more likely to produce a strike." The workers were solidly opposed to a shutdown, he said. This analysis may or may not have been correct. Considerably later, the top leadership had trouble keeping the lower ranks from forcing a strike. In any case, the Abel people very quickly sensed they might be drifting into a dangerous position.

They hit back with the charge that management was behind the strike talk. Working through friendly publications, they said that management was putting out propaganda to support the friend of management—McDonald. This was not true. Management bent over backwards to avoid the slightest partisan move. Even in the most private, off-the-record talks, company bargainers could not be pressed into expressing a preference. They realized that the barest hint of favoritism would be the sting of death for a candidate. Apart from this, there was probably no wild enthusiasm among management people for McDonald or any other union man. "We don't care who's across the table," they said. "All we want is to see this thing settled one way or another."

Yet the companies obviously had a tremendous stake in the election. What was being debated was the manner in which collective bargaining should be conducted. The method the companies had worked so long to develop was being tossed out the window but management could only sit there stone-faced and mute. The only public comment on the election came long afterwards and it was possibly a matter of retrospect. In October, R. Conrad Cooper said McDonald had "exposed his political flanks" by displaying "true labor statesmanship."

The companies did deride some of the Abel arguments during the campaign. No matter who won, they said, the union would still have to rely on staff people like Ben Fisher and Marvin Miller. There were just too many technical questions for anyone to negotiate or administer a contract without specialists. For the most part, however, management was bound and gagged during the election. That was one of the ironies of the whole thing.

As it was, the Abel forces said strike scare talk was emanating from management. In addition, Abel quickly set out to build a peace-loving image. "By bringing rank-and-file sentiment more directly to bear on the bargaining table, we can avoid the kind of communications breakdown which, under McDonald, produced two of the three longest strikes in the history of our union." McDonald had lost touch with the rank and file, they said. This meant management had no good reading of worker feelings. Strikes had resulted because management has miscalculated the temper of the union.

To ensure both good communications and "peaceful progress," the Abel team proposed two changes—the wage-policy committee should be given a running account of bargaining developments, and the wage-policy group should authorize a referendum of workers before any strike was called. The referendum idea, said McDonald, was "foolish." What happens, he said, is that "the so-called last offer on which the balloting takes place is not in fact the companies' best offer." The companies, he said, would hold back, not wanting to shoot their wad on an offer that was certain to be rejected.

In the campaign windup, Abel and McDonald appeared on Meet the Press. Abel had earlier declined a McDonald challenge to a series of public debates. He had turned down the TV invitation at first but then accepted rather than have McDonald appear alone. It was thought this would be a golden opportunity for McDonald. With his

144

long experience with TV, his colorful appearance, and his eloquent speech, he figured to slaughter Abel.

It didn't turn out that way. Abel was no ball of fire on the program. A good part of his time was spent explaining the procedure for handling ballots in the Chicago district. Instead of coming directly to union headquarters, they would be cleared through some district office. Abel said this was a past practice of long standing. But if his opponent failed to generate sparks, McDonald was less inspired. He got into a long quibble on the mechanics of calling strikes. He appeared to shrug off questions. He gave the impression of being complacent and evasive.

How much difference any of this made is a question. On February 9, voting went pretty much along the lines indicated in organizational tests. McDonald was a little stronger in Chicago than had been expected. Abel did better on the West Coast than expected. But in general, the initial pattern of support was holding up. The early reports from the two camps varied widely. McDonald's count showed him winning. Abel reported a landslide for Abel. One of the problems was that neither could get good dope from locals in the other's territory. The next day, however, wire service reports showed Abel leading by a small margin. This was as high as 15,000 in the one count. Later it was down below 10,000. There never was a complete neutral check.

One thing was clear enough. The union was splitting almost down the middle. It could be weeks before even the nominal winner was known for sure. Charges of fraud were already being heard. In Gary, Indiana, McDonald people claimed that Abel people were "doing all they could to steal the election." An effort was made to have votes of the big U. S. Steel local impounded. This was turned down at first. Later, a federal judge did lock up the ballot boxes.

District Director Bill Hart charged irregularities in Philadelphia, a McDonald stronghold. Hugh Carcella of Philadelphia said Abel could have a local-by-local check "provided it's done by the American Arbitration Assn. and also provided Mr. Hart will give me the same consideration in any district I choose." In Pittsburgh, McDonald people were reported heading for Canada "to see what's holding up the vote there."

The election left both sides claiming to have won with neither side in control. Moreover, there was every prospect things would continue that way for an indefinite period. The locals had until February 19 to mail their ballots to Pittsburgh. The union tellers had until May 1, the day contracts expired, to report their findings. That was just part of the problem. Under the Labor Management Act of 1959, a union election protest could be carried to the Secretary of Labor. A complaining member had first to exhaust the union's internal appeal procedure. If there was no final decision in 3 months, the Labor Department then was allowed 60 days for investigation. If the Labor Department found significant fraud, it would first seek some voluntary adjustment. As a final resort, it could file a civil suit to force a new election. Of more than 200 cases filed in the first 3½ years of the act, only 13 had gone to court and only 11 new elections had been ordered. There had never been a case involving a national election of a union as big as the Steelworkers.

The way it looked, it would take 3 to 6 months just to get through preliminary appeals and investigations. If the case went to the courts, it might be 2 years before an actual trial. All of which meant the political fight was very much alive. The McDonald people vowed they would carry their battle through to the bitter end. The Abel people now regarded themselves as official winners of the election. "I think an extension would make sense," said George Meany

146

from Florida. Abel said it was "premature and prejudicial" to talk about extensions.

The government said very little. It did supply two Labor Department officials to travel with the union tellers in hearing appeals and to be on hand for the final vote count. That was the way things stood with the strike deadline only a little more than 2 months away. Two officials with different ideas and bitter feelings each claimed to be the union's chosen leader.

The companies had earlier been given a demonstration of the dangers of trying to negotiate with a divided union. On January 26, negotiations between the Steelworkers and the can companies—American Can Co. and Continental Can Co.—had been broken off in a huff. "It has become apparent," said the companies, "that the union's current internal situation complicates any joint efforts to complete an agreement at this time."

Albert Whitehouse, who was running on the McDonald ticket and who was in charge of talks for the union, said the negotiations had been torpedoed by the Abel people. "Forces supporting Mr. Abel have deliberately attempted to prevent an agreement from being reached. They have gone so far as to threaten company representatives with years of reprisal at the local level if the companies should go foreward with a good faith effort to conclude a prompt, peaceful agreement." Abel called this talk "preposterous" and the companies denied they had been threatened. Nevertheless, the perils of negotiating with a divided union were clearly shown. If management tried to please one side, it could alienate the other.

All this had happened before the election, of course. Now the actual votes were in and there was no point in anyone trying to rush or block a settlement. Talks with the can companies resumed in New York on February 23. The next day the companies offered a 3-year package with a

16¢ wage increase, more SUB, and new pension benefits. The union came back with a demand for 24¢ in wages plus full pensions for 30-year men, regardless of age. For 10-year men, the union asked SUB payments for 2 years. The companies said "No."

On March 1, 36,000 Steelworkers walked out at plants of American Can Co. and Continental Can Co. The companies assailed the union for an unnecessary strike. The union assailed the companies for waiting until the last minute before offering anything and then coming up with a proposal that was "totally inadequate." The McDonald people blamed the can companies for pulling out of earlier talks and were in the mood to let management sweat out a shutdown. "They could have had a deal in January," said one union man. Apart from this, it didn't appear the political fight was creating any big bargaining problems.

On March 22, agreement was reached by Continental and the Steelworkers. A 40-month contract provided about 26¢ in wages, part of which was retroactive. Pensions were hiked from $3.25 a month to $5.50 a month for each year of service. SUB duration was increased to 5 years for 10-year men and 2 years for 5-year men. There was an income protection clause similar to that of the Alan Wood Steel Co. There was a liberalizing of pension benefits for men retiring early but the normal retirement age remained 65.

Cost of the package was estimated at 45.7¢ by the union. Immediately, there was speculation that a pattern had been established for the steel industry. The companies vehemently rejected this suggestion; the auto pact and the can contracts had nothing to do with steel. A top union official went along with this. "The can settlement establishes neither a ceiling nor a floor," he said.

The contract terms smacked strongly of Dave McDonald's total security concept. The fact that the Abel forces had made no objection to this encouraged the belief that the union might be pulling itself together for bargaining. There was one footnote to the settlement. On April 1, D. B. Weisley, vice-president of American Can Co., announced that new labor terms made it "imperative that there be an increase in our container prices." Even though the union's calm bargaining with the can people was not entirely discouraging, the big test was yet to come. In basic steel the full union organization would be involved.

It was March 1 before enough smoke had settled to even talk of resuming the steel bargaining. That day R. Conrad Cooper called on the union to meet the following afternoon and get things going. He said there should be an extension but he said the companies were ready to negotiate. McDonald replied that the union was ready to meet March 8. "We insist on the same format that was used when talks broke off January 7." This meant more mass meetings.

On March 9, exactly 1 month after the Steelworkers election, talks did resume at the Penn Sheraton Hotel in Pittsburgh. U. S. Steel's bargaining room was done up with commercial displays aimed at bringing out the competitive challenges to steel. The meetings were mob scenes. At one of the U. S. Steel sessions, a union grievance man had to be forcibly ousted. He was not on the bargaining team but said he wanted to be there in "case Mr. Tomko overlooks something." Apart from money problems, said Conrad Cooper, you had "hundreds of contract issues and thousands of local issues in the hands of about 600 negotiators in 10 separate company and union groups. . . ." It was a "monstrosity," said the steel official—a "menagerie."

The two sides milled around until, on March 16, the union presented an eight-page list of its noneconomic demands to U. S. Steel. These tightened the tentative provisions on subcontracting and work by foremen. They contained a clause restricting the reduction of work crews.

The demands called for streamlining of the grievance procedure and measures to deal with grievance backlogs. There were provisions on split schedules, safety, and service with the Peace Corps. The union said there would be subsequent demands on vacation scheduling, incentives, job classification, apprenticeship, seniority, and training.

This seemed to indicate things were at least getting organized. Also encouraging was word that a coalition bargaining team had been formed by the union. At one point, there was a move by the Abel group to oust McDonald as chief bargainer. This failed but it was agreed that Joe Molony, the apparent winner of the vice-president race, should be added to the top bargaining group. Also added was James Griffin, director of the Youngstown district and manager of McDonald's campaign.

Along with these were the union's officers—McDonald, Hague, and Abel—plus Marvin Miller and the union's counsel, Elliott Bredhoff and Dave Feller. Abel was made chairman of a subcommitte to draft noneconomic demands. Joe Molony was put in charge of a committee on money demands. This was possibly a tactical move by McDonald to make sure his opponents could not sit back and snipe at his conduct of bargaining. Whatever the motive, the new arrangement seemed to assure some degree of bargaining unity.

On March 29, a month before the strike deadline and 3 months after contracts had been reopened, the Steelworkers presented their first set of economic demands. These included: two general wage increases of 12.5¢ an hour, an added 10 per cent for all jobs not covered by incentives, cost-of-living adjustments, and a guarantee that men transferred to lower jobs would get 95 per cent of their old pay. Six new pension provisions were included. There were four SUB demands—two on sickness and accident—and eight dealing with insurance. Finally, there was a batch of miscellaneous items.

The early speculation was that these proposals might be worth as much as 55¢. Later Charley Allard of the *Pittsburgh Post Gazette* learned that the companies were pricing the package much higher—at more than $1. Union people at the time said it was impossible for anyone to hang any maximum tag on the demands. Many of the proposals were completely general; they called for such things as increased life insurance or longer SUB.

However, the list was formidable enough to bring a very emphatic "No" from chief company negotiator R. Conrad Cooper. "The candidates having promised all things to all people," said Cooper, "the demands put forth by the union wage-policy committee totaled up to new wage and benefits costing somewhere in the neighborhood of $3 per hour for a 3-year agreement." There was one conspicuous omission from the union program. Nothing was said about early retirement, which had been such a big thing in the auto settlement. However, it appeared that the union had done a pretty comprehensive job otherwise. The same day, the Steelworkers supplemented their original list of noneconomic demands with a 9-page rundown on job classification, seniority, and training.

Talks of the individual company teams were continuing meanwhile. Subcommittees had been formed to coordinate these while the top committee was supposedly dealing with straight money manners. Gradually, however, it became apparent that nothing very positive was happening. First, the union's money demands were rejected by Cooper. Then, reports from company talks were discouraging. "We're going over job transfers for the third time," said a company bargainer. "Our people are getting tired."

A more common complaint was just the opposite. Companies claimed that the union was thinking up new gripes faster than old ones could be disposed of. One of the difficulties involved the classification of problems and demands. The companies claimed that many of the so-called local demands involved the master agreement. "We are not going to agree to a tighter contracting-out provision than U. S. Steel," said one mill. Likewise, the companies said all demands were economic—they cost money.

In line with this, the companies said they would not make straight money concessions only to find they were faced with a new set of demands at the local level. They were not going to be faced with the local strikes of the auto industry following a money agreement. It was up to the union's leadership to take responsibility for the full package, said company people. Until there was a leader who was willing and able to tell local people what they couldn't have, there could be no real bargaining. And this ultimately was the real problem, concluded the companies. The union was still too divided and stirred up for real collective bargaining.

The union argued that it was not possible to wrap up all demands in a nice neat package. It was pointed out that the companies differed in size, structure, and problems. Inland Steel, with all its operations in Chicago, had a full seniority plan written into the master agreement. Most of the others had separate plant agreements. Wheeling Steel had a less restrictive past-practice provision than most of the others. At U. S. Steel, there was a special problem related to size. Workers complained that their paychecks, coming from a central computer, gave too little information. Youngstown Sheet & Tube had negotiated separate expiration dates for some of its fabricating operations.

According to a union source, however, the real distinction involved volume and intensity of gripes. Jones & Laughlin had a backlog of something like 1800 unresolved grievances. Great Lakes Steel was another company with special difficulties. On the other hand, companies like Wheeling Steel had practically no serious plant problems. A big difficulty, according to one USWA official, was absentee management of some companies. All problems would be bucked up the line. Cost-cutting programs would be put through without trying to solve the human questions arising. "You may profit by day-to-day decisions," said the union man, "but you wind up with tough demands for contract changes." He mentioned one particular company. "They can't assume because they're in the 11-company group that they'll get a contract with the others."

I. W. Abel was among those who tended to favor decentralized handling of plant problems. "To our way of thinking, it would be to the benefit of both management and the union if more problems could be worked out in individual company talks. A lot of these problems should have been handled on a daily basis at the plants. That's what we've been saying right along." The companies couldn't see it that way. The union leadership had promised the sky to local officials, they said. Now nothing would satisfy the locals. The companies had no assurance of peace no matter how much money was offered.

"What they're trying to do is give everybody two cuts at the ball," said one company official later. "First you negotiate with the International and then you have to satisfy the local." Also much later, Conrad Cooper was to refer to the "unwillingness or absolute inability" of the USWA leadership to make a deal on its own. He seemed to be saying that the union could not make a contract stick with its own people without outside backing. If local officials were stirred up, said the union, it was simply mounting frustration at management's failure to deal with problems. And the locals were stirred up.

In April, a group of eight local presidents met with Abel

153

and called for the union to demand early retirement. This seemed like a minor sidelight at the time but it pointed up the unrest in the ranks. By this time, it was obvious that nothing very good was happening. The companies said the union was still playing politics and trying to please everyone. The union said it was management that refused to bargain. "It looks as though people are starting to regard a strike as inevitable," said a management man in early April. "Nothing is happening," said a Steelworker. "It's just ponderous procedure."

There was further jockeying within the union. Abel was elevated to the rank of cochairman. Various subcommittees were formed. The real question now was not whether a contract could be negotiated but whether an extension could be negotiated. "The question is whether you can develop a posture of negotiation," said a USWA man. The mood of the union was uncertain. "If you're going to fight, sometimes it's better to fight and get it over with," said one top officer.

Abel had indicated that any extension would depend on the amount of movement by the companies. But the way things had developed, it appeared that an extension was dictated by the complete absence of movement. The two sides were so far apart and things were so confused that there seemed no point in a shutdown. Bargaining positions had not been established clearly enough for pressure to do any good.

On April 15, the companies proposed an open-end extension to run at least 60 days after May 1. Some type of benefit was to be included. When this was rejected by the union, R. Conrad Cooper cut loose with a public blast. Since the start of the political fight, he said, the companies had had trouble dealing with a "house divided against itself." The union's first demands had not come until nearly 4 months after its wage-policy meeting. The demands were a "preposterous assembly of proposals arriving at the bargaining table obviously as the result of a massive union force with divided leadership." On top of this were contract and local demands that would mean "an abdication of management responsibility."

As a way out of this "unbelievable situation," the companies had offered an extension plan. "To our union friends, we say the time to meet our obligations and discharge our responsibilities is now." The real problem, insisted USWA officials, was the companies' unyielding attitude. "They keep talking about a crisis, but they keep right on with this brinkmanship. They won't offer anything until they're absolutely forced into it."

On April 19, negotiators were joined in Pittsburgh by William E. Simkin, director of the Federal Mediation and Conciliation Service. On his arrival, Simkin was asked if talks were deadlocked. He said, No, he didn't think they were deadlocked. His perfunctory comments were blown up into a big display of optimism. In Washington, a more positive statement came from Labor Secretary W. Willard Wirtz. Wirtz predicted a peaceful, moderate agreement. "I would expect that the settlement in the steel industry would be within the general pattern which is suggested."

The same day, Dave McDonald announced he was calling the union's wage-policy committee for a strike vote. McDonald said the companies' offer had been "totally inadequate." At 5 P.M. on April 19, the union countered with its extension proposal. This called for a wage increase of something over 17.9¢ an hour. A little over 13¢ of this was related to the government's 3.2 per cent guideline. Another 4¢ was provided to compensate for past increases in cost of living.

This was bluntly and flatly rejected by the companies. The news stories at the time played up the fact that the proposal was based on the federal guideline of 3.2 per cent.

The stories called the plan a 1-year extension. "The union's proposal was neither," said R. Conrad Cooper. It cost about 18¢, he said, which was 4 per cent of steel employment costs. Also, "the union would be free to strike at any time on or after August 15 this year." Further benefits would not take effect until 1966, he said, but the companies could be struck in 3½ months.

On April 20, the companies proposed an extension until January 1, 1966, with a 60-day reopener. This was to be accompanied by "substantial improvements in pension and insurance." On April 21, the companies said the least the union could do was offer a straight day-to-day extension with a 15-day strike notice. The union said "No." On April 22, the Steelworkers wage-policy committee authorized a strike, saying the industry seemed "determined to force a shutdown."

In Washington, a presidential aide was queried on a possible Taft-Hartley injunction. "We would assess the situation in case circumstances arose that might indicate such action," he said. In Pittsburgh, Bill Simkin was saying there wasn't really much he could do if the parties really wanted to strike. Federal mediation was entirely noncompulsory, he explained. It involved "attempts to persuade without any authority to decide." Any kind of binding arbitration called for special authorization from Congress. This could only come after the expiration of a Taft-Hartley cooling-off period. There was no clear doctrine on when Taft-Hartley should be applied.

That was the way things were going into the weekend of April 24. The companies were seeking a relatively long extension—6 months or more. The union wanted the strike deadline advanced no further than August. The companies wanted a floating deadline. The union wanted to limit the reopener to no more than a week or two.

The companies were offering some indeterminate amount,

156

said to be about 5¢ but never really nailed down. For any long-term settlement, management was still talking 2 per cent. The union was talking at least double the "lousy nickel" for a short extension. Its ultimate demands were for about 18¢ a year. On the question of a day-to-day extension, management opposed any retroactivity. "There is no pressure on the union to bargain with retroactivity." The union wanted retroactivity—figuring there was no pressure on management otherwise.

On Monday, April 26, things still seemed hopelessly deadlocked. "It looks tough," said a top union bargainer. That was in the morning. At noon, he said the same thing. Shortly after noon, McDonald and Cooper met alone. Before this, all meetings had included Abel along with Heath Larry of U. S. Steel. The private session was later explained as a mix-up in arrangements. Abel was skeptical ("He ducked me") and was among those surprised by what came next.

A long time before, McDonald had explained his concept of collective bargaining. A bargain was made, he said, when two men sat down together in a room and agreed. That afternoon, McDonald and Cooper sat down together and came out with an extension agreement. Some observers felt this was McDonald's finest hour. With a distinct possibility that his own days were numbered, he could have sat back and said, "Okay, you guys know so much. Let's see you straighten this one out." Instead, he asserted his authority and cut through an impossible stalemate. This was the first time there was real man-to-man bargaining. It was not to establish a precedent.

The new arrangement extended the strike deadline 4 months until September. There was a 30-day reopener. The union had to serve notice August 1 if it wanted to go out September 1. An interim payment of 11.5¢ an hour was to accumulate in escrow for later disposition. The companies noted this was a 2.6 per cent boost. They said it was being given "without prejudice to whether employment costs in a period to be covered by a successor agreement will be either greater or lesser. . . ."

The payment, said Dave McDonald, is "not a measure of the final settlement." It provided "minimum retroactivity —it sets the floor for future bargaining." President Johnson praised the negotiators for the "statesmanlike agreement." "I think we can be confident," said the President, "that the final settlement will be a responsible one which fully considers not only the interests of the immediate parties but also the public interest." A. S. Glossbrenner of Youngstown Sheet & Tube said he hoped to see "an agreement we can live with." I. W. Abel said the union had proved it was united.

For several hours on April 28, this last point seemed very much in question. On noon of that day, a group of local union people began agitating in the lobby of the Penn Sheraton Hotel. Led by Anthony Tomko, president of Local 1408 near Pittsburgh, they circulated a leaflet calling for rejection of "the tin cup agreement." The leaflet noted the packages won in the auto industry and by dockworkers. The last three steel settlements, it said, "have been the thin dime in the tin cup. We have had enough injustice and demand justice. . . . and by God, now is the time." The paper noted, among other things, the "fat pensions" doled out to USWA leaders with short service. The sponsors of all this were the same people who had agitated earlier for early retirement provisions.

At first, it seemed that it was just a case of a few guys letting off steam. Then the move to reject the contract gained momentum. Dave McDonald was cornered in the hotel lobby and given a bad time until he broke loose. Union people were saying the spring was the time to strike

—not the fall. When the wage-policy meeting started that afternoon, it looked as though the local officials, who numbered 130 in the 163-man group, were solidly against the agreement. Speaker after speaker got up and talked against the extension.

Loitering outside behind potted palms were worried management people. The thing they had feared and talked about seemed to be happening—the leaders had lost control of the union. An agreement negotiated by the leaders was being rejected. The union officers played the whole thing cool. They let the dissidents talk themselves out. They postponed the vote and then gradually worked to turn the tide. McDonald spoke in favor of the agreement. Abel talked for it. Joe Molony, who is possibly the best of the union's many fine orators, outdid himself.

Having made their own pitch, the officers quickly called for a voice vote and carried the day. Abel subsequently played down the dissent, saying this was not chaos but democracy in action. Nevertheless, it was a close thing. "If we could have gotten a vote 45 minutes sooner," said a local official, "we would have defeated it." "You can't afford to have another last minute crisis," warned another union man. "These guys are determined to assert their power. They're going to want time to consider any proposal."

"There will be no need for another crisis in steel if the companies share our faith in the process of genuine collective bargaining," said I. W. Abel on April 30. This comment came as he was acknowledging a teller's count that officially awarded the election to him by a margin of about 309,000 to a little under 289,000 for McDonald. Abel's prepared statement did not suggest any feeling that the bargaining structure was in need of tightening or streamlining. His promise was to marshal the "full resources of

159

leadership at every level of the union." The time had come for changes "through which the rank and file can exercise its rightful control."

This was fine political talk, said management, but dammit, you couldn't negotiate with 1 million steelworkers. The elected representatives had to take responsibility and show leadership. Abel didn't see it that way. Could you have bargaining without full power in the hands of the leader? "You do the best you can. You report regularly. The same exercise takes place on the other side of the table. Industry bargainers must report back. They get authorizations from time to time."

But could the Steelworkers leader control and limit the demands of local officials? Abel said, "I think people are reasonable. Some people don't understand the labor movement. People shout: 'If you don't have one-man rule, you have anarchy.' Some publications said there was anarchy at the wage-policy meeting. That wasn't anarchy; it was an example of democratic process. They complained in 1959 about labor dictators. They should make up their minds whether they believe in the democratic process."

This was a good point. In strike situations, management would picture peace-loving workers being ordered to strike by labor bosses. It didn't occur to some management people that the lack of the big boss could work both ways. A weak leader might make easy demands. On the other hand, it might turn out the leader was too insecure to turn down unreasonable demands of the membership. This second possibility was later to cause concern in other fields. "The return of more voice and authority to membership from their authorized representatives creates an impossible situation," said T. L. Hewitt, director of industrial relations, Vulval Mold and Iron Co., Latrobe, Pennsylvania.

Hewitt was discussing contract talks completely removed from the basic steel negotiations. His company had

160

negotiated a contract with local union officials and International representatives. Union members voted against the agreement and went on strike. The only issues mentioned, said Hewitt, were things like letting foremen play on the union ball team. "Throughout the strike, the local union officers were unable to express any real reason for the failure to ratify. Most complained about the capriciousness of the membership. Is the local union membership ready for a voice in union activities?" asked Hewitt. "The majority of the members do not have the background to comprehend the settlement." His particular contract was ratified on the third try.

In the steel industry, bargainers faced the possibility of trying to satisfy two presidents, 163 wage-policy members, 700 local presidents, and half a million workers. The official election returns April 30 indicated it might not be quite that bad. Abel would become the one official president June 1. However, McDonald and his supporters vowed they would carry their fight to every court of appeal. It didn't seem likely they could bring any quick reversal of the official vote. If McDonald followed through with his fight, however, he could keep things in a divided, uncertain state indefinitely.

But the tide was running against McDonald. Several of the directors who had supported him were said to be urging that he step out. Labor Department officials indicated privately they had no intention of rocking the boat by intervening in the election. The charges of fraud all involved technicalities, said the government men. No evidence of clear-cut cheating had been presented. This was possibly true but the feeling was the Administration was not too keen on doing anything that would prolong the union fight. In any case, the handwriting was on the wall for McDonald. He was 62. If he retired, a portion of his pension would continue to go to his family in the event of his death. If he died in office, there would be no pension for his family.

Instead of promptly withdrawing, however, McDonald preserved his bargaining power by insisting he would make a fight. Within the Abel group, there was one faction that wanted to clean house on the opposition. There was a move to oust James Griffin, the Youngstown director. Others were reportedly due for the axe. McDonald held out for general amnesty. Despite powerful opposition to this, the moderates in the Abel camp agreed to let bygones be bygones. This suggested Abel might not be a captive president after all.

On May 19, McDonald announced he was withdrawing protests and bowing out. "I believe . . . that a union which is united behind its new president will be a better union than the only alternative now possible—a union divided by many, many more months of bitter political struggle." He then made a pitch for his philosophy. The Steelworkers had progressed because they had believed in the "leadership principle." The union's president had been given the "responsibility and the power to deal responsibly with the industry. . . ."

He made a plea for the technicians and the new techniques. "If there is any deficiency in the labor movement generally, it is in its reluctance to employ the best brains and the highest talents available. We must develop new approaches and new weapons. . . . We must retain the skills and the technical abilities of the staff." Abel promised there would be no recriminations. People had exercised their free choice. That was their right.

So one big headache was out of the way. Now, at last, the union could settle down to normal. Or could it? In New York, the Steelworkers were negotiating with the aluminum companies. On May 20, the union presented a set of demands that included two wage increases, a doubling of pension benefits, and retirement on full pension for men with 30 years service.

On May 26, the companies came back with a contract calling for 16.5¢ for 1 year. This was promptly rejected by the union. At that point, a fight broke out within the union team. One negotiating group felt the company's offer should at least have been considered. The 16¢ proposal was roughly in line with what had already been negotiated with the can companies. The 1 year term meant new pension programs could still be negotiated in 1966.

One other point was possibly important. The union had fairly good relations with Alcoa, which was doing most of the negotiating for the aluminum industry. There was no big backlog of plant problems. The union considered the aluminum people more flexible and realistic than their counterparts in steel.

One reason for the better relations was that aluminum companies did not have incentives, which were a constant irritant in steel. And in a number of key operating areas, the companies were free to make unilateral decisions. There was no appeal to outside arbitrators. At the same time, the union was free to strike against these decisions at once. This seemed a rough method of settling disputes but it meant things had to be resolved one way or the other on the spot. There was no long period of delayed justice.

At any rate, some of the USWA negotiators felt there should have been some talking about the offer. Others said, No, business was good now. If demands were delayed a year, there was no way of knowing what the economic climate might be. Among the conciliatory faction were some of the top staff people who had supported McDonald. They complained not just about their opposition but about the fact that the top officers would not intervene.

This was galling to the staff men. They had been accused during the campaign of trying to seize too much power.

Now, the people who had done the accusing seemed to be backing away from the tough problem. "I won't make the decision," said one staff man. He said he had tried repeatedly to contact Abel in Pittsburgh and had gotten nowhere.

Finally the International acted. A few days before the June 1 strike deadline, Joe Molony arrived in New York. Molony took hold quickly. There would be no extension, he said, and no 1-year agreement. The company proposal provided too little time and too little money for solving wage and security problems. "We finally convinced the companies we meant business," said a union man. "Joe Molony was the one who did it."

On May 31, with the strike deadline hours away, a 3-year agreement was signed with Alcoa. It provided two wage increases. Taking effect immediately was a 10¢ hike; on June 1, 1967, there was to be an increase of 7¢ an hour. With 2¢ provided for preserving the spread in job rates, these boosts averaged 12¢ and 9¢ an hour. Effective June 1, 1967, pension rates were increased to $5 a month for each year of service. This was roughly double the old rate. There was a supplement of $100 a month for men retiring before they were eligible for social security. Men already retired were given an extra $15 a month.

Finally, the aluminum contract permitted men with 30 years service to retire at their own option regardless of age. This was the point that had been omitted in the original steel proposal and had been demanded by local officials. The full contract was priced at about 50¢ over 3 years for a yearly cost increase somewhere in the neighborhood of 4 per cent.

In the same breath it was announcing the agreement, Alcoa said it was raising prices of fabricated products by varying amounts up to 1¢ a pound. According to Alcoa people, the company president, John D. Harper, was called by President Johnson and told not to be another Roger

Blough. Harper supposedly would have none of this and the increase went through. Reynolds Metals Co. and Kaiser Aluminum & Chemical Corp. followed in both the labor pattern and the price increase. Federal mediator Simkin acknowledged the aluminum settlement was above the government's 3.2 per cent guideline. However, he noted that recently the aluminum package had been "relatively modest. Under the circumstances, I think it is a responsible settlement."

There was no official reaction in Washington to the aluminum price increase. One story said the Administration was "dismayed." While the settlement had been over 3.2 per cent, it said, aluminum productivity had been moving up very rapidly. The one bit of encouragement for the companies was that Molony had been able to pull the union together in aluminum talks. Again, however, this had been a case of dealing essentially with a single company—Alcoa —with 13,000 workers involved and no big mess of plant problems.

The big test would come in basic steel with its mass of people and problems. And there was no sign the new union leaders were ready to back away from the policy of broad participation in talks. At the installation meeting, Abel promised to encourage "our members to play their rightful role in all the basic decisions of this union." This thought was seconded by Joe Germano, the powerful Chicago director. "I'm sure our new officers will agree there is a spot for any of us who want to make the union better. . . ."

Even assuming that internal order could be established, there was still the big question of how much should the companies give. The 18¢ proposal came to 4 per cent, according to management. This number was underlined by the aluminum settlement, which was generally figured at something over 4 per cent. The companies were offering 2 per cent. The Bureau of Labor Statistics had also endorsed 2 per cent. This presented the Administration with a problem because it was in the position of endorsing a ceiling the union would never accept. At the same time, it had called for a noninflationary settlement.

The difficulty was solved on May 3 when the Council of Economic Advisers came out with a special report on steel productivity. Using multiple regression and other advanced techniques, the Council arrived at a number squarely in the middle of the company and union positions. Steel labor costs could be increased 3 per cent without raising prices, it said. One of the big points made in this study was that operating levels had to be considered in any reckoning of productivity. A drop in volume would tend to obscure efficiency gains. A rise in volume would give an inflated picture. There was much more—the effects of a steel price increase on other prices, on foreign competition, and on profits were discussed.

On May 3, Roger Blough recited the industry's position. "Costs must be competitive for they are recovered from only one source—the customer; and the large single element in costs is labor cost. . . ." "They're wrong," said A. S. Glossbrenner of Youngstown. "I agree with what Roger Blough has been saying. The industry has not been retaining enough out of its sales dollar to meet modernization needs." Inland's Joe Block said the CEA recommendations would "either freeze the industry's earning capability or cause further deterioration."

A strong blast came from the chief executive of Republic Steel on May 12. "If you get the idea that we don't like the report, you are right," said Tom Patton. He said the guideline doctrine had no legal sanction. He said 3 per cent was wrong—that it neglected past steel slumps and overlooked the contribution of capital. In the middle of labor negotiations, he said, the views of a third party were being intruded.

166

He said steel prices were not all that important—steel sales were only 2.6 per cent of gross national product.

U. S. Steel later issued a definitive attack on the new guideline. The guide constituted "an obvious attempt by government to pressure wages and prices in the steel industry." The new figure went against the official Bureau of Labor Statistics number. The report stressed benefits to the company with high volume but failed to consider adverse effects when volume dropped. In discussing foreign competition, the report neglected the fact that imports were being dumped. The report exaggerated the importance of steel prices in the economy.

The Steelworkers were equally unhappy with the 3 per cent guideline. Dave McDonald, who was still in the picture in early May, repeated that productivity was only "one of about 14 factors involved in wage determinations." McDonald did note that the study showed steel productivity had risen 4.9 per cent a year from 1961 to 1964 while steel labor costs had gone up only 2.5 per cent.

Another union official was more blunt. "No government is going to tell the Steelworkers what kind of settlement they can have," he said. He recited the union's answer to the guideline. Steel productivity had been moving up at about 4 per cent in recent years. Recent settlements had been modest—2 and 2.5 per cent. The government was wrong in assuming no increase in living costs. The 1964 inflation called for 3.9¢ in added Steelworkers pay. And as long as there was no limit on profits and dividends, there should be no ceiling on wages.

There was one fairly interesting note on the CEA guideline. In reporting the study, news people took their pencils and multiplied 3 per cent by $4.40 an hour—the steel employment cost at the time. The answer came out to 13¢. It was concluded from this the companies would have to come up from 8¢ or 9¢ to 13¢ in order to please the government. This layman's interpretation proved to be slightly naïve.

Round one of the negotiations left the steel companies in an isolated situation. Wheeling Steel Corp. had dropped out of the 11-company group when it looked as though a strike was due for May 1. Wheeling was in miserable shape financially. Its new management, which came from other industries, didn't think too much of the way steel mills handled their bargaining. "Steel is the only major industry that bargains industrywise," said Robert M. Morris, president of Wheeling.

He said it was ridiculous for the industry to keep blaming everything on labor costs. "This raises a question of how smart has the industry been. Shouldn't somebody take some responsibility?" In any case, Wheeling notified the union it was splitting off. That was on Sunday, the day before the extension agreement. This timing pointed up how sudden and surprising the agreement was. Either that or there was a communications breakdown in the company group.

When the companies were meeting after the extension, many of the bargainers still did not know Wheeling had broken ranks. "Where's Wayne Brooks?" asked someone. Brooks was Wheeling's chief negotiator. McLouth Steel Corp. also went off on its own. Like Wheeling, McLouth promised to give any benefits eventually negotiated by the joint group. In addition, it extended incentives and agreed to an extensive new training program. McLouth had never been part of the joint group but it was a big producer of carbon sheet. Its protected status would hurt the other mills in the event of a strike. Wheeling was also a sheet steel producer and would be in a position to pick up business from mills on strike.

The joint group had originally included 12 companies.

Kaiser Steel had dropped out in 1959. Allegheny Ludlum had later withdrawn. Pittsburgh Steel Co. was added but now Wheeling had left. The industry was down to 10 companies. The can companies had signed. The aluminum companies had signed. The government had put an official floor under demands. More and more, the mills were being hemmed in and cut off.

During the extension period, talks continued in an uneventful manner. The union's team was headed by Abel, who was still a questionmark in the eyes of management people. With him was Joe Molony, a jut-jawed Irishman who talked with a slight brogue and who was possibly the most colorful figure in the new lineup. Molony was an alert, articulate bargainer. He did a lot of the union's talking in negotiations.

The new secretary-treasurer—Walter J. Burke—replaced Howard Hague on the union team. James Griffin, the McDonald supporter, remained. In addition, there were the two carry-overs from previous bargaining—Marvin Miller and Elliott Bredhoff, the union's counsel. Dave Feller, who had been counsel along with Bredhoff, stepped out.

The companies had the same four men: Cooper and Heath Larry of U. S. Steel, H. C. Lumb of Republic, and Russell Branscom of Bethlehem. Larry was possibly the most personable of the steel group. He has since been moved up as assistant to Roger Blough. Union people consider Larry a competent, meticulous corporate executive. "Lefty" Lumb of Republic is a tall, rumpled looking man. Son of a traveling preacher, he went to school in North Dakota, starred in sports, and studied abroad as a Rhodes scholar. Lumb is the most informal member of the company team. Russell Branscom of Bethlehem is a dapper, self-contained little man.

With the top lineup stabilized, the two sides plugged

169

away at their mountain of problems. The full bargaining teams were sent home for a while. Various committees met and talked and sifted.

"They haven't accomplished a thing," said a steel president on July 1, the day subcommittee reports were due. "They can't agree on costs and they can't agree on which issues are important and which should be thrown out." On July 12, the approximately 600 bargainers returned to resume full-scale negotiation. By July 16, reports were still negative. There had been no discussions of straight money matters. There was still no real agreement on major contract issues. By then, it was evident there would be a strike notice August 1, and talks would go down to the September 1 deadline. "I think we'll get a settlement midnight August 31 without a strike," said a company negotiator.

At this point, there was still no formal demand and there was no formal offer. It was understood the union wanted something like 18¢ a year; it was known the companies were holding to a 2 per cent position. But things hadn't jelled to the point of a measurable gap. "If it were that simple, it would be easy," said a company official.

He explained that some divisions of his mill had completed their talks on plant problems. However, many of the problems had been classified as economic matters and referred to the central committee. The local union's attitude on local programs would depend on what it got out of central talks. Likewise, the company would be influenced by what it had to concede in the top talks. "Nothing's wrapped up," he said. "Nothing's wrapped up until everything's wrapped up." The companies wouldn't talk money until they knew everything else that would be asked. The union was still committed to giving the locals full voice and full satisfaction.

Conrad Cooper gives this version of what happened next: "With the critical date of August 1 upon us, the

170

union leaders disclosed their real entrenched position—namely the wage and benefit program achieved in the aluminum industry—said to cost close to 50¢ an hour in aluminum but if translated to steel it would have cost upwards of 60¢ or over $100 million per year." There is some question as to the companies' response to this proposal. The union emphatically denied that any new offer was forthcoming. There were reports, however, that something in the neighborhood of 11 or 12¢ was proposed. Whether this actually happened, it was assumed—in the words of a union official—that "Cooper had 11½¢ in his pocket."

In any case, the two sides were as far apart on money as they had been in April. The union's wage-policy committee voted July 30 to serve a strike notice. The policy statement acknowledged that there had been progress on "many local issues and minor contract issues." But there was no constructive response, it said, to the important income and security issues. The companies had moved "only insignificantly" from their 2 per cent position. Abel explained that this movement was the 11½¢ interim benefit rather than any new offer.

Economic needs "cannot be met or even considered intelligently so long as the companies stick to a ritualistic, hopelessly inadequate, penny-pinching stance. Indeed, we are beginning to wonder whether the cumbersome bargaining machinery utilized by the companies permits achievement of satisfactory settlements within reasonable negotiation periods." The union noted it had gotten a quick settlement when it negotiated with one aluminum company—Alcoa. It hinted it was thinking about going back to single company talks in steel.

So the strike notice was served. The steel industry, which thought it had gotten away from crisis bargaining, now faced its second crisis within 1 year. The union blamed the companies for both. "Too often," said Abel, "management is reluctant to do right away what they know they will do ultimately."

R. Conrad Cooper's response was fairly mild. Enough headway had been made on contract and local problems so that these fall in line "if the parties could settle the hard-core problem, namely—how much?" The companies were willing to offer a fair share of progress "but the union felt impelled . . . to insist upon more—about twice as much." Cooper said there had been attempts to find whether "there is an area between us that would be reasonable and on which there could be a basis for agreement." Abel said there had been "discussions of various types of approaches."

This was the kind of maddening talk that reminded reporters of the Human Relations days. You could explore a position without being committed to an offer. Some sources said flatly there had been a 12¢ offer. The union flatly denied there had been any offer, formal or informal; nothing had been mentioned beyond 2 per cent.

With 1 week gone in August, the word was the same: no progress, no change. "It's going down to the last week in August," said a union source. "It's a bad dream." On August 13, it was the same story. "We meet," said the union bargainer. "We shuffle papers. Nothing happens." It was learned that the two sides were arguing about cost estimates. "Even if your figures are right, you're not in the ballpark," a top company man told the union.

On August 18, Federal mediator William E. Simkin arrived in Pittsburgh. He met with companies' officials that night. The next day, he conferred with the union. "I have every hope and believe that there will be a settlement," he said afterwards. He would not characterize talks as dead-locked. His presence should "not be construed as inter-vention." The Administration was not "unduly jittery." Talk about strike measures was "very speculative." Sim-kin's arrival seemed to be the signal for preparing preliminary "final" positions. From the start, people had said the steel fight would be settled in Washington. This belief made it logical to protect positions until the final intervention. Now the Administration had made its first move.

On Friday, August 20, one of the steel bargainers was asked why the companies had never made some kind of new offer. "We have made an offer," he said.

"You mean the 11¢ or 12¢ people were talking about at the end of July?"

"This was more than 12¢," he said.

He declined to say how much more but it seemed reasonable to assume that if it had been—say 2¢ more—he would have said more than 13¢.

So *Iron Age* magazine came out with a special release: The companies had made a new offer believed to be at least 13¢ an hour or something close to 3 per cent a year. The next day an official union statement branded the story "pure speculation." Privately, union officials were just as discouraging. "There has been no offer," said Walter Burke, USWA secretary-treasurer. "Cooper is willing to so stipulate." So the company source was asked again: Had there really been an offer? Certainly, he said. There had been a written offer and a number of the company people thought it should be out in the open. They were pushing for a public announcement.

The following Wednesday—August 25—the companies announced they had presented a package they valued at more than 13¢ a year. For 35 months it came to 40.6¢. "This would raise employment costs at the rate of 3 per cent a year." said the announcement. This seemed to confirm the earlier story except that the companies said the offer had been made not the week before but the day before. The important thing, though, was that there had been a new offer.

It provided two wage increases—one for 10¢ to 21¢,

the other for 6¢ in the third year of the contract. This was reasonably close to the aluminum pattern of 10¢ the first year and 7¢ the third year. The companies estimated the wage provisions would cost 22¢ an hour. In the second year of the contract, the companies offered a pension program, and in the third there were added insurance benefits. No details were given on the pension package, but it was believed to provide a boost in minimum payments from $2.50 a month to $4.50 a month. This again was within shouting distance of the aluminum scale. Most important of all possibly was the companies' estimate that the increase would raise employment costs 3 per cent a year. This seemed to mean management was complying with the guideline specifically devised for steel bargainers.

The union immediately answered that the offer really only amounted to 37.1¢. It was not for 35 months but for 39. On this basis, it came to only 2.3 per cent of employment costs. Some of the union's arguments were not too serious. The Steelworkers said the companies were out to cut incentives. Privately, union officials admitted this proposal was confined to one company—U. S. Steel—and that it involved a standard "buy-back" offer. In return for a lump sum, the company could reduce an incentive it considered out of line. Also doubtful was the union contention that vacations would be taken away. At the time, USWA officials said the only changes discussed involved options for trading vacation time for extra pay.

But there was very serious disagreement about pension costs. Both sides later acknowledged there was no way of predicting just how much new pension benefits would cost. It was unfortunate that this type of benefit arose in negotiations that were difficult and tangled to start with.

Also unfortunate was the confusion about contract timing. The union argued that costs should be reckoned against a period starting May 1. Steel productivity had been increasing during the 4-month extension period, they said. It was ridiculous to invoke a standard based on yearly productivity and then leave out part of a year. The companies said the extension had explicitly excluded any retroactivity. The new contract would take effect September 1. Terms could only be valued against a period starting on that date and running for 35 months.

There was another serious problem not directly related to guidelines. Management, said the union wanted to "sweep under the rug many unresolved contract and local issues." This was unquestionably true. The companies did want a cutoff on plant gripes. R. Conrad Cooper had indicated there were no insurmountable problems left in this area. It appeared that many local officials felt a lot of important demands had yet to be satisfied. This was possibly the most fundamental aspect of the statement. Although Cooper played down plant problems at the time, he was later to question whether the union's leaders could make any agreement stick with its own people. Whether correct or not, this estimate meant that management wasn't sure the most lavish money terms would satisfy all union echelons.

In any case, there was a stalemate. Federal mediator Simkin couldn't budge the two sides. Senator Morse could not get any action. Finally, the problem fell into President Johnson's lap. The President summoned bargainers to Washington August 30. By 8 P.M. that night, an 8-day extension had been negotiated.

On Tuesday, August 31, there were "amicable and intensive sessions." Senator Jacob Javits (R., N. Y.) said the strike threat showed the need for broader presidential powers in dealing with labor disputes. He urged prompt hearings on a bill that would let the President order a 30-day freeze with provisions for a fact-finding study. He said the President should also be empowered to seize struck facilities in the interest of national health and security. This was the kind of a proposal that could always be expected in a steel crisis. It was one of the things the companies had to consider in their final stand. If they resisted informal persuasions, they might find themselves facing some type of official regulation.

Presidential press secretary Bill Moyers emphasized on Tuesday the Administration was providing only informal assistance. Wirtz and Connor were acting as "catalysts. . . . It's collective bargaining in the truest sense of the word." "Secretary Connor and Secretary Wirtz exerted every possible effort, objectively and impartially, to help the parties resolve the issues by collective bargaining," said Conrad Cooper afterwards.

During Tuesday and most of Wednesday, it didn't seem that this kind of mediation was enough. Bill Moyers said there was "hard, tough bargaining." No progress, said Joe Molony of the union as he returned for dinner Wednesday. That night, however, there was a report that the companies had raised their offer by 2.5¢. This story, which appeared in the *New York Times* the following morning, was officially denied by the union. "No new offer has been tendered," said Abel on his way to the White House Thursday morning. When pressed, other union officials admitted there had been movement. "There is a basis for the story," said one negotiator. "We had some constructive talks, but it's like pulling teeth."

What happened was that the companies did offer 2.5¢ more to raise the job classes of skilled craft workers. But at the same time, they reduced the increment in their general wage offer. This was the kind of thing that made for conflicting reports. Also confusing to outsiders were the various ground rules. During the aluminum talks, a company bargainer denied an offer that everyone knew had been made. "Under our rules," explained a union man, "an offer is no longer an offer once it's rejected. It's as if it had

176

never been made." In the steel situation, the general rule was that "nothing was settled until everything is settled." And carrying over from the Human Relations days, nothing was firm until everything was firm.

Another danger was that reports were colored by the viewpoint of the source. If you asked one union bargainer what the companies were doing, he would invariably say nothing. That might literally mean nothing. Or it might mean nothing in relation to what this particular official thought they should be doing. Yet it was gradually dawning on people that one thing had been settled: there wasn't going to be a steel strike. "We'll settle," said Charles Beeghly of Jones & Laughlin. Cornered at breakfast in the Carlton Thursday, Beeghly spoke with smiling resignation. The companies would settle, he said, because, if they didn't, it would be settled for them. Some sort of fact-finding board or commission would hand down terms after a lot of palaver. The companies might as well do right away what they would be forced to do eventually.

At the White House, President Johnson seemed to agree. The President talked for about 40 minutes to negotiators Thursday. He told them an agreement could be made "right away." He strolled over to the White House and told reporters he had given negotiators a "few pious thoughts." These were mostly a review of an Economic Advisers report. The points made included: (1) A 2-month steel strike would have as much impact as a recession of 8 or 9 months; (2) steel pay had risen 188 per cent since 1954 and was 33 per cent above the average for all manufacturing; and (3) steel profits in the first half were up 36 per cent from the previous year and 100 per cent from 1961.

Mr. Johnson seemed thoroughly genial and relaxed through all this. He said Mrs. Johnson had been contacting him daily about plans for the Labor Day weekend. He said he hoped negotiators would wind things up soon enough to spend their own holidays with loved ones. This reference to holidays and families was a nice twist of the screw for men who had been living with their problems for months. However, there was nothing threatening in Mr. Johnson's public manner. He had not reached the point of presidential edicts. "I know you've got problems," he reportedly said during the recent maritime strike, "but end it."

Finally, Mr. Johnson and Bill Moyers repeatedly stressed the independence of the bargainers. "Abel is a very able horse trader," said the President, "but he may have met his match in Cooper." "These are tough, tenacious men," said Moyers. The plain fact seemed to be that President Johnson was enjoying himself immensely. His energy amazed the bargainers and possibly convinced them they had no chance of outlasting him. And the grind was telling on many of the others.

The President stepped up the pace on Thursday. Instead of allowing a break for the evening meal, he had both lunch and dinner sent in. It was announced that the bargainers would work straight through. A little after 6 P.M., however, the union team came straggling into the Statler. Pausing over a refreshment, one of the Steelworkers admitted there had been some action. "We've come down," he said. How much? "Below 49¢." A big part of the union's movement throughout talks involved special rates sought for men not on incentives. Originally, demands called for bonuses for all men not on tonnage incentives. This was eventually pared down to only a few skilled classes. Also, there were adjustments of the various pension offsets.

While the union was coming down on Thursday, the companies were going up. Their offer on pensions was raised from $4.50 a month to $5.00 a month. The last point to be settled was early retirement. The union was demanding full pensions for 30-year men, regardless of age. Union

178

officials said this would cost a little over 2¢ an hour, a figure they arrived at by arbitrarily doubling an estimate made for the early retirement program of Alcoa. The companies said there was no way of predicting the cost but that it would probably be a lot more than 2¢.

Just when this final issue was resolved is not known, but by Thursday the companies were offering most of the essentials in the Steelworkers pattern. President Johnson had said there could be an agreement right away. Reporters at the White House did not see how there could be enough money difference to keep the dispute going much longer.

Yet, there was no agreement. The parties worked till about 1 A.M. Thursday night without settling. Friday morning went by with still no word of a signing. "The reason for the failure was recognized," said R. Conrad Cooper, "namely, union leader unwillingness or absolute inability to settle except at government request." Joe Molony once quoted Phil Murray on the functions of a labor leader. It was his job to fight for the rights of the workers; it was also his job, Murray had said, to tell the men the things they couldn't have. Management still questioned the will or the power of the new union leaders to tell their people which demands had to be discarded.

Late Friday afternoon, the government gave the extra nudge, the outside backing, or whatever it was that had been needed. "In an extreme effort to be helpful," said Cooper, "Secretary Wirtz and Secretary Connor then made recommendations with respect to each issue. Reluctantly, we agree to accept the proposals."

"Neither side was fully satisfied," said the union, but under all the circumstances, it was decided the recommendations "constituted a reasonable basis for resolving the economic issues." The alternatives, said Cooper, were "a devastating, costly steel strike . . . or official government intervention or some other form of third-party participation

179

with ultimate resolution entailing consequences of unknown magnitude."

"We had three things staring at us," said a steel staff man, "congressional action; a Taft-Hartley injunction; and the sentences coming up in the antitrust cases." These cases were the ones involving sheet products. No-contest pleas had been accepted and the companies had been fined. Still pending were sentences for William E. Stephens, Jones & Laughlin president, and James Barton, manager of sheet and strip sales, U. S. Steel. Price-fixing is a criminal offense. The two men could have been handed jail terms and fines up to $50,000. There was no sign the government was approaching the price cases in a punitive spirit. The no-contest pleas had gotten the companies off the hook as far as civil damages went. Similar pleas had been accepted in the smaller actions. But if the companies had stood on their private-enterprise rights in the labor talks, there could have been the spectacle of a public plea for freedom while two leading steel officials were jailed for tampering with free processes.

More important than the price cases was the general influence of government. Steel men emphasized there had been no threats by the Administration. Yet, there was a built-in threat for the companies. "It's not necessary for power to be brandished for it to have an effect," said a steel president later. But there was no ranting against the government then or later.

Both sides were probably happy to have their arms twisted. And that was the hell of it. After years of complaining about intervention in wages and prices, steel bargainers found themselves in a situation where intervention was "obvious." "Maybe it means we've become some sort of public utility," said one steel official. "It means we've got to do better next time," said Lefty Lumb of Republic. "We did sign it," said Heath Larry of U. S. Steel when asked if the settlement had been dictated.

Actually, there was no occasion for dictatorial extremes. The agreement ceremony showed how far the whole thing was from a serious confrontation. There was again a wait of an hour or more while TV time was lined up. There was no worry about stopping a shutdown but the weary bargainers were gasping for air. "We just wanted to get home," recalled a union man. Instead, they were entertained by the President. He talked constantly during the wait. There was one serious discussion in this period. Mr. Johnson's original TV text said something about the settlement being squarely in line with the guidelines.

The wording had a familiar ring. An *Iron Age* story earlier had noted that the company's 3 per cent offer seemed to be squarely in line with the special steel guideline. R. Conrad Cooper may have recalled the 1962 experience when the steel industry allowed another agreement to be called noninflationary and had then increased prices. He objected to the President's text, saying the point about inflation was controversial. A union official suggested a less explicit wording. The text was softened.

On TV, Mr. Johnson said this: "The settlement is a fair one. It is designed to prevent the inflation which would damage our nation's prosperity. It is also within the guiding spirit of the collective bargaining in a free country." Following the telecast, the President detained his guests while he rummaged through desk drawers looking for souvenir pens and other mementos. He spoke on the phone to Mrs. Johnson in Texas. He had Mrs. Johnson say a few words to Cooper, who was slumped down in a chair. He talked to the negotiators.

On this low key note, the 1965 steel negotiations ended. A strike had been avoided and that was no mean accomplishment. At times during talks, it looked as though there could never be a settlement. The union seemed to be coming apart at the seams. The companies were refusing to budge. There was a settlement but every other bad thing happened in 1965. Instead of a quiet agreement, the bargainers had gone through two noisy crises. There had been the biggest inventory buildup in history and the biggest influx of foreign steel. The final settlement had been a full public spectacle with television coverage and headlines.

Moreover, there was no great promise of better things to come. The settlement left both sides feeling put upon. The union's wage-policy committee okayed the terms but only after some loud grumbling about problems being sidestepped. There were warnings that next time we'll take 'em on "one by one." The Human Relations clause was officially deleted from the contract.

The Steelworkers, said Cooper, were a "massive force." Because of its excessive power, the union could create a national crisis. It could force government intervention. "The reasoning seemed quite simple—what could they lose?" Cooper complained not only about the union's demands on basic steel but its insistence that the basic steel pattern be forced on small mills and little fabricators. He closed by referring to the need for legislative surgery on "the obese body of labor union power."

The union responded in kind. How could Cooper call the union obese, asked Abel, when it was worth $21 million and the 10 companies were worth $9 billion. "The giant steel corporations for which he speaks have grown large and powerful over the prostrate bodies of many other small, independent steel companies. . . ." The charge of rigid pattern bargaining was a "deliberate untruth." Cooper's whole attack was "vicious and unwarrented."

In short, the two sides were not off to a running start in their effort to do better the next time.

1965 · A NICE GUIDEPOST FIGURE

The steel people said the contract was inflationary. The government said it wasn't. Had there been a deal? If not, how would the mills react to guideline price control.

The labor settlement left one big question to be resolved: What would happen to steel prices? Throughout negotiations, President Johnson had made two stipulations—there was to be no strike, and the settlement should be non-inflationary. To many people, these were mutually exclusive aims. If management resisted demands it considered inflationary, there would be a strike. If management offered enough to avoid a strike, there would be a price increase.

One theory was that the Administration would sacrifice its price objective in the interest of peace. It would give the union what it wanted but then tell the companies privately to go ahead with price hikes. There would be a deal. This theory was shot down by the President right after the settlement. On national television, Mr. Johnson made it clear to all he did not consider the terms excessive and would not stand aside for a price boost.

183

This thinking was underscored September 9 by Gardner Ackley, chairman of the Council of Economic advisers. The settlement would cost 48¢, said Ackley; this amount should be figured against a contract term of 39 months (not the 35 months used by the companies). "On this basis," said Ackley, "48¢ comes out to a nice, guidepost figure of 3.2 per cent."

According to the companies, it was too nice and neat. They charged that Ackley had worked backwards, starting with 3.2 per cent and assigning a value to early retirement that would make the total come out right. The companies also argued it was ridiculous to take a contract that was dated September 1 and use a term that began May 1. The union was equally skeptical of Ackley's reckoning, even though his figure was just a shade higher than their own estimate of a little over 47¢. "We've been working for months on this thing," said one USWA bargainer. "We have some idea what it will cost." No one, he said, could pretend to have a precise estimate after a few days study.

Privately, both the union and the companies admitted there was no way anyone could predict the cost of early retirement. The amount would depend on the number taking the retirement option and the pension levels of those leaving. However, the union figured something over 2¢ was a very safe maximum. A number of the companies used 5¢ as an unsafe minimum. The standard provisions of the contract were valued by the companies at 46¢. With early retirement, the total cost was figured at more than 50¢.

"How this can be declared compatible with the so-called guidelines or how it can be characterized as noninflationary is a little beyond my ken," said A. S. Glossbrenner of Youngstown Sheet & Tube on September 28. "It's perfectly clear we have been saddled with a very substantial increase in labor costs," said L. B. Worthington of U. S. Steel on September 29.

184

On October 14, R. Conrad Cooper said the contract would cost "somewhere above 3.5 per cent." Early retirement costs could not be estimated in advance, he said. The government's reckoning was a "pea-and-shell game." "No matter how you slice it," said Cooper, "the settlement will exert heavy upward cost pressures."

So there it was. The government said the contract was noninflationary. It "points the way" to wage-price stability, said Secretary Connor on September 23. The companies said the cost was about double the justified amount of 2 per cent. There seemed to be all the elements for a price showdown—a confrontation.

There was just one piece out of place. In his definitive review of negotiations October 14, Conrad Cooper appeared to release all the frustration that had been building for nearly a year. He had seen the Human Relations program go down the drain. He had watched his 2 per cent guideline get kicked sky-high. Now, he lit into the Steelworkers as an obese body and a massive force that made collective bargaining impossible and preyed on small companies. It was possibly the strongest blast in the whole stormy history of steel-labor relations.

But in this tirade, there was a strange note. All references to the Administration were sympathetic and even appreciative. Intervention had been forced by the union. Administration officials had been impartial. The final recommendations had been made in "an extreme effort to be helpful." All this seemed completely out of character for a steel industry spokesman. For years, steel men had deplored every form of government intervention. In 1965, there had been the most blatant and persistent kind of intrusion.

Before talks started, the Administration had told the mills there must be no price increase. In the middle of negotiations, at a time when the mills were offering 2 per cent, the government had endorsed a 3 per cent package. When the

185

final intervention came, the union got practically all the essentials of its basic economic pattern. Although the cost exceeded the specific 3 per cent guideline, the Administration blandly pronounced the terms noninflationary. In evaluating the package, Gardner Ackley accepted the union's argument that the term of the agreement should include the 4-month extension period.

Nevertheless, Conrad Cooper had only nice things to say about the government. Cooper did reject the low cost estimates but he carefully avoided any criticism of Administration actions and officials. It looked as though U. S. Steel was playing a deep game. Whatever that plan was, it clearly did not include a clash with the President of the United States. Not if this could be avoided.

On October 13, it looked as though a way had been found to get the price relief steel men wanted and avoid a big public fight. On that date, U. S. Steel announced a tinplate increase of 25¢ a base box (217 sq. ft.). At the same time, it reduced uncoated can stock by as much as 45¢ a base box. The uncoated material was only used in a small number of can applications. However, the can companies and the mills had been trying for years to get away from tin as a coating material. Because of remote, limited supply, the tin price was highly volatile and shortages were always a threat. Prior to the October move, the price of tin had almost doubled.

In August, American Can Co. had come out with a specially designed tin-free container. U. S. Steel's price cut tied in nicely with this development. In this setting, the price cut for tinless steel was more important news than the increase for tinplate. Moreover, there was every justification for the hike. Tin prices had skyrocketed. Tinplate had not been included in the round of increases in 1963. The new thin-gauge products had brought big savings for users

186

and created tough cost problems for the mills. The Administration could hardly object to this kind of isolated price increase, accompanied by a price cut and backed by all kinds of cost justification.

Actually, a pattern of piecemeal increases had been developing for some time. The mills had increased galvanized sheets and a few pipe prices at the tail end of 1964. These moves drew frowns from the Administration and there was a brief lull. Then on February 16, Crucible Steel Co. of America raised the price of carbon die steel in small sizes by 4¢ a pound. On May 8, Latrobe Steel Co. put through an increase of 8¢ a pound for high-speed steel and certain types of hot-work die steel. At almost the same time, Allegheny Ludlum announced increases of $4 to $9 a ton for intermediate grades of electrical sheet.

All these moves were distinct from earlier ones on tonnage steels. The electrical grades and the tool steels were specialty products. They were made for the most part in small, cold-metal shops. There had been no general increase for electrical steel since 1958, said Allegheny Ludlum, and "there have been five general announcements on improved quality guarantees." Specialty mills were particularly hard hit by raw-material increases because they did not have blast furnaces and were entirely dependent on purchased supplies.

"These things have come one at a time," said E. F. Andrews, purchasing vice-president for Allegheny Ludlum. "Put them together and you have a big increase." "Tungsten goes up and down like a yo-yo sometimes," said J. E. Workman, president of Latrobe Steel. "The final straw was the price we had to pay for molybdenum from the stockpile." Workman made the point that specialty mills had a high labor content in their product. "It's pretty difficult to automate for a 200-pound order," he said. "It's certainly different than the tonnage business." Specialty producers argued that they were in a distinct business and their price moves had nothing to do with increases for carbon steel.

Nevertheless, the March changes did lend continuity to price push. They helped establish the new pattern of limited increases, spaced over decent intervals and limited enough to avoid a confrontation. On March 31, Crucible Steel boosted the price of cobalt-bearing magnets by 5 per cent. On April 27, Roger Blough said he knew of no "out of the ordinary price change which we contemplate in the immediate future."

On May 3, Joslyn Manufacturing and Supply Co. initiated a 7 per cent increase on stainless bar and billet. This was just about when the Administration was coming out with the report that said steel labor costs could be boosted 3 per cent without a price hike. On May 10, Inland Steel made some adjustments on secondary sheet prices. The same day, Wheeling Steel increased manufacturing terne plate by 95¢ a base box. This is a very minor item, made by few producers. Secondary sheet is reject material, also of minor importance.

On June 16, Commerce Secretary Connor said the steel industry "should—and will—take the public interest into consideration when they consider prices." On July 3, U. S. Steel increased the heat-treating extras on plates, rods, bars, and certain wire products by $3 to $15 a ton. From a volume standpoint, this was one of the most significant moves since 1964. It raised the price on a good portion of the tonnage of alloy steel produced in this country. On July 15, U. S. Steel increased the price of long terne sheet by $6 a ton. This is a lead-coated sheet, made by a limited number of producers, but fairly important from a tonnage standpoint.

At approximately the same time, Republic Steel announced that on August 1 it was revising the quantity extras on all sheet products. Formerly there had been no premium for individual items of more than 20,000 pounds. The minimum was raised to 30,000 pounds. At the same time, the minimum order quantity was reduced from 40,000 to 30,000 pounds.

This move attracted considerable attention because of the importance of the products involved. However, it was impossible to really measure the impact. For the large auto and appliance makers, it meant nothing. "We've always refused to pay these quantity charges," said one purchasing agent. Presumably some accounts would be affected or the change would not have been made. The mills said the change was not designed to make users pay more but only to make them order in decent quantities.

In early August, Allegheny Ludlum reduced some stainless base prices but revised quantity extras at the same time. At some time in this period, plate mills increased flange quality and fire box quality extras. Thickness and burning extras for plate over 1½ inch were boosted by one mill. On August 15, U. S. Steel put through a price cut when it eliminated the physical quality extra on sheets. There were other price cuts sprinkled in with the increases. Apart from formal changes, there was daily bidding for big stainless steel orders. Just what net impact this movement had could only be surmised. One national news story, which broke in the final days of negotiations, suggested the mills had already gotten a generous slice of price relief through the series of individual changes.

Steel leaders obviously thought otherwise. On April 5, Tom Patton of Republic said recent "moderate and selective increases" had barely offset "numerous price decreases since 1958." In view of higher quality, it was "obvious" that prices should be "free to attain levels that afford us an opportunity to earn adequate profits."

On April 26, finance chairman Robert Tyson of U. S.

Steel also noted that price cuts had outweighed price increases. In the past 12 months, he said, the government's steel price index had declined three-tenths of a point. Near the end of June, C. M. Beeghly of Jones & Laughlin warned that price increases would have to be considered if the steel-labor settlement followed the aluminum pattern. "Commercial factors would have to be considered," said Robert E. Williams, executive vice-president, Youngstown Sheet & Tube. "I don't think an across-the-board increase could happen," said E. J. Hanley, president of Allegheny Ludlum. "I feel most firmly the market is the determining factor. In the early summer, Inland Steel chairman Joseph Block warned of the need for price hikes to permit an "adequate return on capital."

Steel men felt they had obtained a piddling amount of price relief before the settlement. It was all very good to put through increases in drips and drabs. This kept the government off your back, but could you get significant relief in this manner? And why should the industry have to kowtow to the government? These feelings were intensified when the settlement imposed what the companies considered an excessive cost burden. However, the only new hikes were on a highly selective basis.

On October 7, U. S. Steel increased the grade extra for special quality plates by $4 a ton. On October 13, there was the announcement of the tinplate increases and reduction. On October 20, Latrobe Steel Co. announced increases for carbon and low-alloy specialties. All this time, sentiment for a major price challenge was mounting within the industry. On October 20, Republic Steel issued a pessimistic earnings forecast. Increased labor costs "will further intensify the cost-price squeeze . . ." said Tom Patton. Prices will go up, said one steel president, "when someone has the courage to raise them."

A key executive put it this way: The labor contract made

it more necessary than ever to modernize. At the same time, the contract was taking away the money needed for modernization. The only answer was a price increase. ". . . in the industrial world," said Roger Blough on October 13, "the right to price is synonymous with the right to live. Steel prices . . . must have the freedom of movement to respond, either downwards or upwards, to the competitive conditions prevailing in the market place." This was the same mouthful Blough had such difficulty with in his press conference following the 1962 increase. In October of 1965, steel users were liquidating inventory and demand was about as weak as it had been for 2 years. If you didn't know better, you would say Blough was demanding the freedom to cut prices.

Thus, it looked as though a big price breakout was in the making. On October 25, Jones & Laughlin announced it was following others in a 2 per cent increase for steel conduit. On October 26, National Steel was "examining its costs even more diligently." The various intimations were possibly not lost on the Administration. On October 21, Arthur M. Ross, a 49-year-old University of California economist, replaced Ewan Clague as head of the Bureau of Labor Statistics. Ross indicated the Bureau would henceforth do more interpretation. The *National Review,* a conservative publication, said Clague's departure might mean "complete politicalization" of the Bureau.

Then on October 29, the Administration showed it was not kidding about guidelines. Olin Mathieson Chemical Corp. raised the price of aluminum ingot 0.5¢ a pound and mill products 1¢ a pound. On October 31, President Johnson asked for a meeting of aluminum officials with the government on disposal of surplus stockpile aluminum. There were sessions November 1 and November 3.

On November 5, Alcoa followed in both the ingot and product increases. Defense Secretary McNamara said the government was going to drop 200,000 tons of stockpile metal on the market. Later, this was raised by another 100,000 tons. Gardner Ackley blasted the increase. There were various representations. "As Secretary of Defense, I am the biggest buyer of aluminum," said Secretary McNamara. He noted that the department would take 300,000 to 400,000 tons in 1966. There was talk of more sinister pressures—probes into aluminum income taxes, defense blacklisting, antitrust actions. The news stories dutifully noted that just rumors of these acts could be effective.

At any rate, Alcoa withdrew its price increases on November 10. After the hard-nosed handling of increases in June, this about-face was a little startling. It's possible Alcoa was brought into line by the stockpile threat. Demand for aluminum was strong but the industry was just pulling out of a long period of price weakness. A sudden imbalance could possibly set things back a year or more. Also, Alcoa was keenly sensitive on trust matters.

There was one particularly disturbing note in the aluminum showdown. The Administration stoutly denied its stockpile releases had anything to do with prices. Apart from the asinine nature of this denial, it suggested a free-and-easy way with facts.

In the steel dispute, the government had moved from 2 per cent to 3 per cent and to 3.2 per cent without batting an eye. When pressure was needed, the Defense Department came up with a statement saying it could not afford to lose a day's steel production. After the settlement, the CEA quickly produced a cost figure that supported its position.

You would expect management to react predictably to any wage question. Any increase would be too much. And you would be surprised if a union said any offer was enough. You would expect partisan reaction from partisans. But you wouldn't expect to be sure of the federal government's reaction on a vital issue. Now, the element of doubt was dwindling. With each crisis, the government response seemed more arbitrary and less judicial. "Lo and behold," said R. Conrad Cooper, "up comes the magic number of 3.2 per cent." "This was an expedient contract settlement," said Allison Maxwell of Pittsburgh Steel, "and we should never lose sight of that fact."

From a practical standpoint, the aluminum rollback meant that the government was going all out to defend its guidelines. This point was underscored in November when a 2¢ copper increase was rescinded at the Administration's request. The copper move involved a stockpile release of 200,000 tons. However, this was not really a tactical move. A bad copper shortage had developed. Producers and everyone else welcomed the added supply. Nevertheless, there had been another precedent and another success for the guideline control of prices.

In the meantime, Arthur Ross, at the Bureau of Labor Statistics, was issuing the first of his interpretations. Wage gains in major contract had averaged 4.2 per cent in the first 9 months of the year. This seemed to mean the 3.2 per cent guideline was being battered at the wage end. No, said Mr. Ross. The wage increases might be a little high in the first year of the contract but in steel, for example, there was no wage increase in the second year. Over the full length of the contract, wage hikes averaged a little over 2 per cent. The inclusion of fringe benefits would raise the cost somewhat over that figure, conceded Ross. He neglected to mention that the 14¢ wage hike in 1965 would be followed by a 2.3¢ increase January 1 and a 1966 pension package that even the union agreed would cost at least 17¢.

In Congress, Senator Philip A. Hart was beating the drums for tougher antitrust legislation. Big industrial concentrations were stifling price competition. The alternatives were either government regulation or laws that would clip the wings of the big trusts. Hart did not explain how government fixing of prices would be the answer to a lack of price mobility. Nor did he explain how tougher price competition would preserve smaller companies and prevent further concentration.

Meanwhile, Armco Steel revealed its employment costs would be up 17¢ in 1966 and Social Security would add another 5¢. This prospect was causing further scrutiny of prices. On December 19, Latrobe Steel boosted tool steel prices 1¢ to 3¢ a pound. "The enormous increases in labor and material costs since the last price change in 1958 can no longer be absorbed," said Latrobe.

1966 · SURE, WE TALKED TO THEM

How far should the government go in guiding price decisions? How far should a company go in cooperating? These were questions for steel men in 1966.

On December 31, 1965, with everyone leaving for the New Year holiday, Bethlehem announced a $5 increase in structural steel. The Administration's reaction was swift and strong. "Our economy cannot sustain full employment without inflation," said Gardner Ackley, "if producers take advantage of strong markets and increased defense requirements to raise prices when profits are already soaring." A later Ackley statement said Bethlehem had given little information to "justify the price increase."

Senator Wayne Morse said Congress should enact wartime controls. "Let us hope that price-control laws will not be necessary to check economic avarice in this war but if companies such as Bethlehem Steel can only be controlled by price laws, then the American people should demand of the Congress that it get busy and pass such a law as soon as possible. . . ."

Representative Emanuel Celler (D., N. Y.) proposed a bill calling for basic industries to give the government 60 days notice of any price increase. Representative Henry S. Reuss (D., Wis.) proposed a congressional review of price moves. Senator Philip Hart (D., Mich.) said he planned to dig into "lock-step pricing." There were various comments on "profiteering." One news story noted that the recent steel settlement had conformed with the guidelines. The Defense Department announced it was shifting business to companies that did not raise prices.

On January 3, Inland Steel announced it was following in the price hike. ". . . structural shapes are among our least profitable products," said Joe Block, "while at the same time being in very strong demand." Colorado Fuel & Iron Corp. announced a $3 increase but then said it would wait a while.

At this point, all eyes turned toward U. S. Steel. The biggest steel company had only to say the word and the price increase would become final. The guideline structure, with its lack of legal backing, would have toppled. From a tactical standpoint, it seemed the ideal time for a challenge. The Bethlehem increase affected a product that was only 7 per cent of total tonnage. Even though the companies had been introducing some increases, the fact was the Administration had seized on one very minor change and made a horrendous fuss.

Steel profits weren't soaring. They rose only 8 per cent in 1965, a year of record volume. Earnings were down to about 6 per cent of sales. Operating profits, which canceled out the effects of tax changes, were up only 5.7 per cent. For steel people, the trend in intervention certainly seemed to warrant a stand. An across-the-board increase in 1962 had been attacked by the Kennedy Administration. Despite the size and scope of the increase and despite the question of duplicity, many people considered the 1962 attack in-

196

temperate. Now a small increase for one product was being blasted and no one considered the Administration's reaction surprising. It did seem that the trend toward guideline control was moving in galloping steps.

On January 5, U. S. Steel made its move. It increased structural prices not $5 but $2.75. It excluded certain heavy sections from the increase. It threw in a reduction of $9 a ton in west coast prices of cold-rolled sheet. "The overall effect of these price actions represents about one-tenth of 1 per cent in the price of all steel produced domestically," said Leslie B. Worthington. "Only through the exercise of price flexibility can American industry discharge its full responsibilities . . . Price adjustments—upward and downward—are a necessity."

The Administration accepted the compromise offer at once. "The action of U. S. Steel is generally consistent with wage-price guidelines," said Gardner Ackley. There was much grumbling within the industry, particularly after it was learned U. S. Steel had talked to the government before taking action. The inference was that the steel company had gotten permission before announcing its change.

"Sure we talked to them," said a U. S. Steel official. "But we had no idea how they would react when we made our announcement." There had been no advance clearance of the increase, he said, and there had been no commitment on future moves.

"We did not abdicate," said the official. The White House confirmed this version. "U. S. Steel did not ask the Administration's consent to its announcement," said Bill Moyers, "nor did the Administration give its consent."

Roger Blough spoke in conciliatory tones. "We can readily understand how the Administration is concerned about price stability. We experienced some satisfaction over the reception that our price action had." Blough also turned loose a few bits of economic philosophy. It was "natural"

197

for companies to try and raise prices in a period of strong demand. Inflation was a problem but "prices cause inflation like wet sidewalks cause rain." This last was an epigram that had been coined earlier by Blough.

Many other steel men groused ". . . only a free market can test the validity of a product on price," said C. William Verity, president of Armco Steel. "I think the government's intervention was wrong, period," said Charles Beeghly of Jones & Laughlin. Joe Block was outspoken in his disapproval. At a Chicago meeting later, he got into a head-to-head argument with Ackley.

One of the many things that irritated the more hawklike steel men was the reduction in west coast sheet. This was regarded as a sop to the Administration. It was the kind of sham that further compromised the pricing integrity of the industry. "We're going to announce a reduction in plates and an increase in sheets," said an official of a mill that made no plate and a lot of sheet.

But in their more thoughtful moments, some steel people admitted that U. S. Steel had probably been smart. "I'm tremendously relieved," said one staff man. The industry could have made a tough stand, he said; it could have had a public triumph; but in the long run, you didn't win a fight with the President of the United States. "In recent weeks, there have been the first flickerings of a sympathetic ear on imported steel," he said.

The Administration's attitude on taxes was critically important to the steel industry. With the economy heating up, economic thinkers were starting to talk about a general tax increase. There was pressure to rescind the 7 per cent tax credit, which was adding close to $100 million a year to steel earnings. Still not finally resolved was the question of how the depreciation status of companies should be judged. Most important, perhaps, was the possibility that informal "jawbone" control might be replaced by formal

198

controls. The Administration was resisting pressure for both price regulation and tax increases. "We are still feeling our way in these matters," said Gardner Ackley on February 1 about the guidelines, "and it may be best not to institutionalize them yet."

Steel men argued that voluntary curbs on prices and spending were not the answer to inflationary pressures. "No matter how diligently and patriotically business and labor try to plug the leaks in the economic boiler," said Roger Blough on February 19, "they cannot succeed unless someone stops pouring on the coal." Government spending on nondefense programs was the real culprit. It was a mistake to curb the economic freedom that was "a unique source of our military and economic strength."

But while talking as positively as ever, U. S. Steel continued to tread softly. On March 1, it announced increases of $1 to $6 a ton in the extras for wide, heavy plate. No change was made in prices of smaller plate. The increases, said U. S. Steel, averaged out at $2.92 or 2 per cent. At the same time, published prices of certain rod and nail were withdrawn. In the future, said U. S. Steel, they would be negotiated "with the objective of competing with imports." This was considered another smokescreen to obscure price increases. There was again grumbling that the industry should not have to stoop to such devious tactics to get a nubbin of price relief. The price hawks really howled when it was brought out that Jack White, a public relations vice-president of U. S. Steel, had advised Gardner Ackley of the proposed price move 3 days before it was announced.

The CEA let it be known that it had been consulted and had given its blessing to the adjustment. This broadcasting of all preliminaries seemed a tactless assertion of power. One of the CEA members, Arthur Okun, complained later that the press played up sensational confrontations while neglecting the constructive work that was done quietly by the Council. The problem was, the Council seemed to go out of its way to make guideline control an official, public thing. Its public blasts of increases implied official authority in price matters. Its blow-by-blow account of the plate episode made certain that everyone knew its authority had been acknowledged.

This last point was jumped on. News stories described U. S. Steel's "surrender." In 1962, Roger Blough had notified the government only as the public announcement was going out. This time U. S. Steel had come with its hat in hand and waited until the government said okay. "I presume if they had said 'No,' the changes would not have been made," said a steel company president.

That was the general opinion. The fact was, of course, that U. S. Steel had increased prices of tinplate, structurals, and plates. It had done this at a time the Administration was rolling back aluminum, copper, and molybdenum boosts. It had gotten important price relief and it had stayed on speaking terms with the Administration. This was certainly quite a trick. Nevertheless, there was grumbling in steel circles.

On March 11, Joseph Block of Inland Steel blasted the government for "an all-out attack on a relatively minor increase." Inland's profits were down 4 per cent because of "substantial increases in our costs with no improvement in the average price of our products." A. S. Glossbrenner of Youngstown Sheet & Tube warned that "prices must be responsive to cost factors." "It is inevitable that steel prices must go up," said Allison Maxwell of Pittsburgh Steel Co. Republic Steel noted that its labor costs had gone up 14¢ in September of 1965. Another 2.3¢ was added January 1 and August 1 would bring a hike of at least 16¢. "This could turn out to be one of the most expensive contracts we ever signed," said an official of another company.

On the other side, government statements and actions

suggested continuing guideline control. On May 2, Gardner Ackley warned businessmen they were making too much money. "It is time to ask whether a further rise in the share of profits in the national income is in the interest either of the health of the nation's economy or in the interest of business itself." Profits had risen 88 per cent since early 1961, said Ackley. The first quarter rise of 12 per cent substantially exceeded "the rise in employee compensation. . . . Does anyone imagine that labor will continue to show moderation in its wage demand when prices and profit margins are continually rising?"

This kind of talk was infuriating to company people. They charged, first of all, that Ackley was picking his spots, comparing profits in the depressed year of 1961 with those in the boom year of 1965. This, by itself, exaggerated the profit gain. Moreover, said management, Ackley was taking only the profit dollar increase without relating it to volume. In basic steel, for example, dollar profits had risen 31 per cent since 1960 but sales had climbed 26 per cent. As a result, the profit share of the sales dollar had gone from 5.7 per cent in 1960 to only 5.9 per cent in 1965. The profit per cent was down in 1965 from the boom year of 1964. It was down from the 1955 boom period. If you compared peak times, profit margins were shrinking rather than "continually rising." And if you were talking about labor-management shares, you should not be using percentages derived from gross profit volume.

Steel people were among those with another beef. Ackley, they said, was taking broad profit and price numbers and applying them to industries that had had no great relief in these areas. ". . . about 62 per cent of the increase in the Wholesale Price Index since July 1964 is accounted for by three categories," said Robert C. Tyson, finance chairman, U. S. Steel: "Food and farm products; nonferrous metals; and hides, skins, and leather products."

The point was that inflation in these specialized fields was being used as a basis for judging wage and price movements of the big, basic industries. Steel prices rose only about 2 per cent from 1960 to the start of 1966. Steel profits dropped from more than $650 million in the first half of 1965 to less than $580 million in the first half of 1966. In relation to volume, profits were considered highly unsatisfactory by producers. Anyway, steel people were whipping themselves up to strike a blow for freedom and justice. "We'll act at the proper time regardless of what the consequences are from Washington," vowed Thomas F. Patton, Republic Steel chief.

On May 16, Joseph L. Block of Inland Steel said guideline applications were "incompatible with our free enterprise system and can cause great injustices to the parties concerned." In this setting, the next move came as something of a letdown. On May 18, Republic Steel did put through a price increase—$2 a ton for special quality bar and semifinished. However, Republic cut merchant bar $1 a ton and shell billets $2 a ton. There was some talk that the merchant bar reduction was related to import competition. Another producer smiled at this explanation. Foreign bar was priced so far below domestic material that the $2 was inconsequential; the price cut could only have been made to mollify the government.

So the steel industry was still treading carefully. Moreover, it received another reminder of guideline control on July 13, when the Administration rolled back a 5 per cent increase for molybdenum. But there was another factor that did not take any reminding. Steel labor costs were going up 17¢ to 21¢ an hour. The exact amount would depend on the cost of early retirement. And the August 1 boost was coming on top of an increase of 2.3¢ on January 1 plus another 5¢ for Social Security.

This was clearly one of the most concentrated doses of

cost escalation in steel history. Coming at a time when steel feelings were bruised, the new pill would be bitter indeed. It was, in fact, too much to swallow. On August 2, Inland Steel Co. announced it was increasing sheet products $3 a ton. This came to 2.1 per cent, said Inland. "Though higher prices could be justified," it said, "we are holding our advances down to modest amounts in keeping with our desire to cooperate with the government's program of price restraint."

The 2 per cent increase for sheet, like those made early in the year, just about bridged the gap between steel reckonings of labor costs and productivity. The mills had said the contract should cost no more than 2 per cent. They maintained it had cost about 4 per cent. The difference was 2 per cent.

This was modest enough but it took in the most important product line of the mills. When all the flat-rolled products were included, they came to something like 40 per cent of total tonnage. Moreover, there was no compensating reduction. It was a clear-cut, undiluted increase. Gardner Ackley tried to get a delaying action started. "May I urgently request that your company take no action prior to discussion with the government," he said in August 3 wires to 12 mills. But this time, the steel people were not waiting for a buildup of pressures. Armco Steel Corp. and Jones & Laughlin Steel Corp. followed with increases August 3.

By August 4, U. S. Steel and Republic Steel had announced increases. The whole industry quickly joined in the move. Bethlehem Steel reportedly did consult the government but for the most part the industry simply presented the Administration with an accomplished fact. There wasn't time for an issue or a confrontation to develop. Ackley did grumble about "irresponsible" action, but the Administration's situation was described very concisely by Bill

Moyers, Presidential press secretary. Moyers quoted Mr. Johnson as saying "no one could force the steel companies to do what they don't want to do." And that was it. When the steel industry said "No" firmly and quickly, the powerful guideline control evaporated.

Various reports noted that the steel increase had caught the Administration in the middle of the airline fiasco. Here, labor had told the world it would not be satisfied with anything remotely resembling the 3.2 per cent guideline. The reports commented on the shrewd timing of the steel increase. Shortly after, there came a flurry of reports that the government had given up on the basic guideline concept. Commerce Secretary Connor said on August 8 there would be a "new look" at the question of whether any rigid "formula" could be applied. Treasury Secretary Henry H. Fowler also had some doubtful words.

These comments were later softened but it did seem that the steel industry had reestablished its pricing freedom. It had shown that if it really wanted to make a boost, there was no way the government could apply restraints. The case was closed. Or was it? On September 8, President Johnson said he was asking Congress to suspend the 7 per cent investment credit for a period starting September 1 of 1966 and running until January 1 of 1968. "Our machinery and equipment industries cannot digest the demands currently thrust on them," said Mr. Johnson. "Our capital markets are clogged with excessive demands for funds to finance investment. . . . A temporary suspension of the investment credit will relieve excessive pressures. . . ."

There was no suggestion that the suspension was a retaliation for the steel price increase. A tax change had been under consideration since the start of the year. The Administration had been under criticism for not acting sooner to cool off the economy. Yet the steel price increase and the credit suspension were not unrelated. The Administration was moving to relieve inflationary pressures. The steel increase had been a conspicuous display of inflation, put through without even the "courtesy" of a call on Gardner Ackley.

If nothing else, the price-tax sequence showed there were always a lot of bad things that could happen after a steel increase. These might be strictly coincidence. In 1962, a price-fixing indictment, which had been in the works for months, had broken just as the mills were trying to justify their price policies. Retribution might be part of the general tide of events. The 1966 credit suspension would probably have come with or without the steel price hike. The point is, it did come immediately after the steel price move. That was something the mills would remember the next time around. And there was no question the mills regarded the suspension as a personal body blow.

The change was called "selective and discriminatory" by C. William Verity, president of Armco Steel Corp. "The heaviest penalty will fall on those companies who are trying hardest to create new job opportunities and to make American industry more competitive with overseas producers." The government was reneging on a commitment, said Thomas F. Patton, Republic Steel chairman. "The suspension of the investment tax credit at this time would be a blow to modernization programs which were planned on the Government's assurance of continuation of the credit."

The move would mean "reliance on additional bank credits or higher steel prices," warned Charles M. Beeghly, Jones & Laughlin chairman. "In the first place," said Roger Blough of U. S. Steel, "this credit is a needed form of depreciation. . . . Second, because of the long lead time, any suspension would be ineffective from the standpoint of having an immediate anti-inflationary impression. . . . Third, it is very likely to have its effect in the fourth quarter

205

of 1967. . . ." With a capital downturn indicated, said Mr. Blough, the actual loss would hit "at just the wrong time."

Finance chairman Robert Tyson of U. S. Steel denied that the nation was facing profit inflation. He said the profit share of national income had dropped from 10.3 per cent in 1950 to 8.2 per cent in 1955 and 8.0 per cent in 1965. On the other hand, said Tyson, employee compensation had gone from 64.1 per cent of national income in 1950 to 67.8 per cent in 1955 and to 70.3 per cent in 1965. His figures did show a reversal of these trends in the most recent years. The profit share was up since 1960 and the labor share was down. This short span, however, compared a bust year with a boom year.

Government spending at all levels had gone from 24 per cent of gross national product in 1950 to 27 per cent in fiscal 1966. Spending had risen $59 billion or 43 per cent since 1960. The defense portion of this had been only $12.1 billion or 27 per cent. Tyson noted finally that most of the inflation was concentrated in a few specialized fields. He suggested, also, that the pressure of overall demand on supply was easing or, at least, getting no worse.

It did seem the tax measure was directed at the worst possible spot. With a need for more supply, it was curbing additions to supply. Greater productivity was needed to meet wage demands and foreign competition. The tax change was cutting off the supply of productive tools. For basic steel in 1965, the investment credit came to around $100 million or something under 5 per cent of capital spending. This was not an overpowering amount but it was enough to be missed. The debt portion of steel capitalization had been creeping up—from around 16 per cent in the early fifties to 22 per cent in 1965. Individual mills were strapped for cash.

In U. S. Steel's case, there didn't figure to be any immediate effect. U. S. Steel had set out to spend $600 million in 1966. It had been physically unable to spend $500 million. If it lost all its tax credit, it would still probably have more money available than it could spend. Finance chairman Tyson acknowledged there was some truth to this. He argued, however, that the credit would eventually have a significant effect. "It's $20 million a year," he said. "Over five years, that's $100 million. "You can buy a lot of beefsteak for $100 million."

At any rate, the steel people did die a little when their price hike was followed by the credit suspension. In the steel industry and in other industries, there was now a decisive shift away from peaceful coexistence. Without further hemming and hawing, management proceeded to really stomp on the price guidelines. On November 8, Allegheny Ludlum announced 2.5 per cent increases for stainless steel sheet and strip. This was hardly a big challenge. Earlier, International Nickel Co. had boosted prices 7.5¢ a pound, or nearly 10 per cent. Nickel is a major alloying element for stainless and it was simply a question of time before the increase was passed on.

Edward J. Hanley was summoned to Washington but there were no fireworks. In telegrams to other stainless producers, Gardner Ackley offered only mild admonishments. We hope you don't boost prices, he said in effect, but if you do, we hope you'll take it easy. There had been no clash, either, when high-speed steels were increased Nov. 4. Vanadium Alloys, which initiated the hike, was summoned to Washington. Other producers received telegrams. The price move was supported and there were no public recriminations. Increases for tungsten-carbide cutting tools were handled in about the same manner.

Then in January came a jumble of moves and countermoves. On January 4, Jones & Laughlin Steel Corp. announced an increase of about $5 a ton for tubular products.

Gardner Ackley hoped "that other steel producers will consider carefully their own and the national interest and avoid a price increase on tubular products." On January 5, Phelps Dodge Corp. raised the price of copper 2¢ a pound—to 38¢. Other producers quickly followed. Gardner Ackley said that "all who are concerned with continued noninflationary economic growth will greatly regret their decision to raise prices at this particularly critical time."

On January 10, Climax Molybdenum Co. announced a 3.7 per cent increase in molybdenum prices. On January 11, Republic Steel Corp. and Pittsburgh Steel Co. said they were coming out with higher pipe prices. The next day, Olin Aluminum increased aluminum ingot 1¢ a pound and aluminum mill products 1.5¢ a pound. Alcoa, Reynolds, and Kaiser quickly upped their prices. "The national interest was poorly served when the aluminum industry today jumped on the bandwagon of metals price increases," said Gardner Ackley.

"I want to assure the American public that this ill-timed sequence of price increases—for tubular steel products, copper, molybdenum, and now aluminum—does not mark either the failure or the end of government's efforts to obtain responsible pricing restraint by large corporations."

But school was out for guideline control of prices. All the products mentioned by Ackley had been hit with price rollbacks in 1965 and 1966. Now, industry was asserting itself and there wasn't much the Administration could do. But again, that wasn't quite true. On January 11, in the middle of the price breakout, President Johnson delivered his State of the Union Message. "I propose," said the President, "a surcharge of 6 per cent of both corporate and individual income taxes—to last for two years or for so long as the unusual expenditures associated with Vietnam continue."

Mr. Johnson did not relate the tax to price increases.

"As 1966 ended," he said, "price stability was being restored." He noted that wholesale prices were lower than in August. During the 18 months since troops had been sent to Vietnam, he said, prices had risen 4½ per cent. That compared with 13½ per cent at the start of the World War II and 11 per cent in the Korean period. So the tax hike did not appear to be an answer to price hikes. Nevertheless, the one had followed the other again. And, again, it was the steel people who registered unhappiness and concern.

Roger Blough of U. S. Steel said the surtax "probably would have an adverse effect on the steel industry and the same kind of effect on the economy." Blough's comments came January 31 as he was reporting a drop in U. S. Steel's earning from $275 million in 1965 to $249 million in 1966. The surtax came with the steel business in a slump and the whole economy running out of gas. The fact was that the economy had been cooling itself off since the previous September, when the Administration withdrew the 7 per cent investment credit. By January, when the President was proposing a surtax, recessionary signs were clearly evident. It was clearly not the time to talk about repressing business.

Despite this picture, there was a great deal of profound gibberish written at the time about the stimulating effects of a fiscal plan that would drain off buying power through higher taxes but would pump deficit dollars into the economy. Nevertheless, steel people had another object lesson in the bad things that can follow a price increase. At the same time, however, other events were demonstrating the folly of profitless pricing.

THERE ISN'T MUCH YOU CAN DO

These events were taking place in the world steel market. In this market, American losses were reaching disastrous proportions. U. S. imports of steel, which had been a little over 1 million tons a year in the midfifties, were close to 1 million tons a month in 1966. Export of steel dropped from more than 5 million tons in 1957 to less than 2 million tons in 1966. American mills had lost out because they steadfastly refused to meet world prices. When imports began rising in 1959, domestic producers argued that wage differentials were the big cause. Foreign wages were one-third to one-sixth the American scale. U. S. labor had simply priced itself out of the world market.

In 1962, with domestic demand depressed and 4 million tons of imports arriving, a new explanation was given. U. S. mills charged that foreign rod and pipe were being dumped in this country. The dumping law says a country can't sell for less money abroad than in its home market. These complaints got nowhere. The Treasury Department did find violations by several European nations but it did not nail the Japanese. Since Japan is the biggest single

210

shipper to this country, it was held that the amount of steel being dumped was not enough to damage domestic producers.

By 1964, steel people were talking about still another problem—the inequity of tariff duties and other trade barriers. Worldwide reductions were being sought under the General Agreement on Tariffs and Trade (GATT). The Kennedy round of talks had been initiated by the Trade Expansion Act of 1962. Steel people urged that trade negotiators consider the total picture, including dumping and such things as import licenses, border taxes, quotas, embargoes, and foreign exchange restrictions. "It is our recommendation," said Leslie B. Worthington on February 19, 1964, "that rates of duty and nontariff barriers should be considered jointly in relation to their overall impact on international trade in steel mill products."

While domestic mills were agitating and protesting, foreign mills continued to eat into the U. S. market. Dumping complaints here brought expressions of lofty indignation abroad. Dr. Herbert W. Koeler, general manager, Economic Community of the Iron & Steel Industry, said U. S. producers were reverting to the old "protectionist" ideas. At a time when everyone else was thinking along global lines, he said, this was a step backward. It did look as though the American industry was trying to wall itself off from aggressive, progressive world competition. Steel men insisted otherwise. "It's a matter of competition with foreign producers who use completely different rules," said a U. S. Steel official. "If you open up the market at all, the rules must be the same for all."

It was not just low prices the mills were up against, he argued. It was dual pricing. A high price at home was used to subsidize low-priced exports. "Their traditional method of marketing steel mill products is to maintain stable prices in the domestic markets," said Henry J. Wallace, sales vice-

211

president of U. S. Steel, "where almost all of them sell the bulk of their production, and then sell the surplus output, based on their incremental costs, at whatever prices they can obtain." This was not progressive, said steel men; it was the same thing American companies had done in the old robber-baron days. The big food chain would jack up prices in areas where it had no competition. It would use the profits to destroy little stores in other areas.

It was argued that in neither situation, at home or abroad, were the foreigners permitting true competition. At home, said Leslie Worthington, steel was sold at "prices which the steel producers jointly seek to stabilize—usually with the aid of their government." The American Iron & Steel Institute later referred to a "permissive attitude toward cartels and other arrangements for establishing minimum domestic prices. . . ."

One steel executive was contacted by a French counterpart after the dumping complaints. "Why didn't you talk to us?" asked the Frenchman. "We could have worked something out." The American explained that it is not good form in this country to hold price discussions with competitors. This was all very uncivilized to the European.

According to the mills, foreign producers went to the other extreme in export selling. "Their present method," said Henry J. Wallace in 1964, "is by under-pricing the domestic producer in whatever amount is necessary to take the customer's order." This amount was running $50 to $60 a ton under domestic pipe prices, said Wallace. "As I view it, this is the practice of predatory pricing," he said, "a practice, I am told, that our laws are intended to suppress." He and others insisted you could not meet this kind of competition. "We found," said Leslie Worthington, "that when we lowered our own price, that the price on the foreign steel was reduced correspondingly."

Underlying foreign practices was a philosophy including

elements of the managed economy and possibly the old feudal system. Foreign governments were involved to a greater extent than our own in steel operations. There were official pressures to maintain full employment and contribute to favorable trade balances. Foreign managements seemed inclined to accept the responsibilities of the old feudal patron. "There's a reluctance to lay people off," said T. A. Wheeler, vice-president, international, Allegheny Ludlum Steel Corp. "If you hire a man, you're going to have him more or less permanently."

In short, there was a tendency to treat labor as a fixed cost. In this situation, there was every incentive to keep production up by cutting prices on surplus tonnage. And the surplus, said U. S. mills, was unloaded in this country. "By marketing his excess production in this way," said Leslie Worthington, "he is able to utilize a labor force which either the law or local practice causes him to maintain, regardless of the need for their services, and he is also able to earn foreign exchange for his government. . . ."

But weren't foreign mills really responding to the market? When demand dropped, they cut prices enough to find buyers. Wasn't that the way the law of supply and demand was supposed to work? No, said American officials. Foreign mills were operating without regard to the level of demand or the state of the market. "The Japanese will sit down and decide they're going to ship 4.5 million tons to this country in a year," said one executive. "There's no discussion of price. It's just decided in advance how much will be sold."

The fallacy in all this, said U. S. producers, was that the market was relatively inelastic. "If customers don't buy steel, there isn't too much you can do about it," said Robert Tyson, U. S. Steel finance chairman, in 1962. "I doubt if you would go out and buy two cars instead of one if the price of steel were cut." With demand fixed at any point in time and with mass production tools that might have double the capacity of a weak market, attempts to maintain peak output could only be destructive. If carried far enough, the process would put competitors out of business and reduce competition. The American response to all this was to vary production with demand. Most steel is produced to order. If the orders don't come in, production is cut.

On the other hand, American prices do not fluctuate. Over the years, Robert Tyson had said, steel operations have averaged 75 per cent of capacity. With steel markets subject to violent swings, he had indicated, you must figure on lean periods and you must have prices that give an adequate profit at the average level. If you don't do this, say steel people, you won't be able to carry the capacity for peak periods. In line with this, American mills sold at the same price to all customers, big and small, far and near. "We in United States Steel believe that it is good business to treat all our customers alike," said Leslie Worthington.

This was a matter of fairness to domestic mills, a matter of conformance to laws on price discrimination and a matter of commercial soundness. "If we started selling sheet at a reduced price to Volkswagen, what do you think General Motors would say?" said one executive. But ultimately, it was the conviction of steel men that an industry with heavy capital costs and cyclical markets would erode if it gave away any part of its production. All of which was fine, but while American mills complained, foreign mills were growing and prospering. Steel imports rose from 4.1 million tons in 1962 to 5.4 million tons in 1963 and to 6.4 million tons in 1964.

The real flood began in late 1964, when users started stockpiling for the 1965 steel labor negotiations. Imports had been running at the rate of 0.5 million tons a month. They jumped to 0.7 million tons in November of 1964 and were over 1.0 million tons by March of 1965. On all counts the domestic reaction seemed to be defeatist. . . . Foreign mills were more modern because these mills had been largely rebuilt after the destruction of World War II. This was a particularly bitter point with steel men because American dollars had contributed greatly to the reconstruction.

"Since the close of World War II," said Leslie Worthington, "our government has provided the money to build, modernize, or expand 179 different foreign plants. . . . this money has reached the astonishing total of one billion, seven hundred and thirty-five million dollars. By way of contrast," added Worthington, "the American steel producer has been able to expand and improve his own steel facilities through his ability to pay his own way." This ability was fairly limited for a long stretch. A slump gripped steel markets from 1958 through 1962. Steel output, which had been above 117 million tons in 1955, never went over 100 million tons in the lean period. Steel operation ranged between 60 and 70 per cent of capacity.

Steel earnings dropped to $600 million in 1962, the lowest since 1954. Capital spending dropped to $900 million, the lowest for any year since 1954 and just about equal to 1962 depreciation. By 1963, the industry was turning out only 8.5 million ingot tons by the basic oxygen process. This high-speed method had been developed in Europe in the early fifties. Nearly 10 years after its introduction, less than 8 per cent of American production was by the new method.

On continuous casting, vacuum degassing, and other new methods, it also seemed that foreign mills were coming up with the new ideas and were showing greater willingness to try unproven methods. The American steel industry appeared as a fading prima donna, sluggish and conservative in technical matters, a crybaby in commercial matters. In

215

the summer of 1963, a slightly different picture began to emerge. While the American market was finally rising from its 5-year slump, demand abroad was losing a little of its steam.

When volume dropped abroad, so did profits. Meyer Bernstein of United Steelworkers found serious concern about earnings at a 1963 meeting of the International Labor Organization (ILO). "They stated categorically that they can't go below 70 per cent and make a profit," said Bernstein. He cited 1960 figures compiled by ILO. Lumping together steel earnings and depreciation, these showed a return on sales of 8.9 per cent in Great Britain, 10.9 per cent in America, and 13.7 per cent in France. Bernstein noted that the American margin was based on operations below 67 per cent of capacity. At this level, he said, the U. S. profitability was considered "astonishing."

At this time, there was apparently no great difference between steel prices here and abroad. One study showed cold-rolled sheet selling for 6.35¢ a pound here, 6.26¢ in Britain, 6.75¢ in Germany, and 6.51¢ in France. This rough price parity was verified by sources like Rockwell Manufacturing Co. and Westinghouse Electric Corp. From a standpoint of material costs, they said, there was no great advantage in operating abroad. All this suggested surprisingly high cost levels abroad. Domestic producers had always implied that, with much lower wages, foreign producers had total costs that were much lower than ours.

This point now seemed open to question but the early reports were received with skepticism here. You couldn't tell anything from foreign financial statements. Companies in Europe kept three sets of books. They often started with dividends and worked backwards in reporting finances. In 1964, however, American steel men began getting some firsthand knowledge of operations abroad. U. S. Steel had become part owner of an Italian operation and was negotiating for an interest in a Spanish mill. Allegheny Ludlum had become joint owner of Allegheny Longdoz, a stainless finishing operation in Belgium. Crucible Steel Co. of America, Pittsburgh Steel Co., and Armco Steel Corp. were among those ultimately acquiring foreign interests.

Along with technical missions, these new ventures gave steel people a better understanding of the other side. "They're not quite as democratic abroad," said Aimes Wheeler, who headed Allegheny Ludlum's international division. There was more family management, said Wheeler. There was a bigger social and organizational gap between top management and operating personnel. "You get quick decisions at the top," said Wheeler. "I think you move slower at the plant level. There is more need to get to the top for decisions. I think they're still behind us in management techniques."

Within home markets, the tendency abroad was toward top management fraternization. If you wanted to sell, you hired someone from a good family who would have contacts with the good families in other plants. Sales and purchasing functions were underdeveloped in Europe. There was more secrecy, less technical exchange, less mobility. The heel-clicking atmosphere had worked against the buildup of a professional management group.

Aimes Wheeler was particularly struck by the financing abroad. "I never cease to be amazed by the debt these people are willing to carry and by the amount the banks are willing to extend. They'll often finance a project over one-half through borrowing." In this country, funded debt usually averages around 20 per cent of capitalization. The mills have been criticized for being too conservative but they can cite the experiences of Kaiser Steel Corp. and Wheeling Steel Corp. These mills went deeply into hock and wound up with deficit operations. With a market that may drop 50 per cent in a few months, say steel men, you simply can't let fixed money charges get too big.

In 1965, a number of things started to catch up with foreign producers. A general slowdown saw West German steel production dropping and very negligible gains in Britain, Austria, and Luxembourg. At the same time, world capacity kept climbing. There was a 50-million ton increase in 1965. Of this, 24 million tons was in the free world and all but 1 million tons outside the United States. By the start of 1966, world capacity exceeded demand by 75 million tons or more.

By American standards, this was not an unmanageable excess. It meant world demand equaled about 80 per cent of capacity. U. S. mills made money with operations between 60 and 70 per cent for 5 years. But foreign mills went into their lean period with big debts and relatively inflexible labor costs. Most important of all they had the tradition of maintaining high operations by forcing surplus tonnage on the world market.

The result of trying to unload 75 million tons on an unwilling market was predictable. ". . . producers offered steel in the world market at lower and lower prices in the hope of maintaining volume," reported the American Iron & Steel Institute in 1967. ". . . domestic prices declined in some countries as home producers, striving to slow imports, aligned on the reduced prices of other countries," said AISI. "Inevitably, this sequence of events has led to sharply lower revenues. . . ."

With world steelmaking on a mass production basis, dumping could not be confined to the other fellow's backyard. It backfired. When this happened, it proved the point Henry J. Wallace of U. S. Steel had argued in 1962. "We know how much it costs to make steel," Wallace had said.

218

"They could never exist if their whole net was the same as their net on pipe sold here."

During 1965, stainless sheet prices dropped 5 to 25 per cent in Europe. "I'm told that no specialty steel producer is making money in Europe," said Joel Hunter, Crucible Steel president. "Two Japanese stainless steel companies went into bankruptcy at the end of 1963," reported Edward J. Hanley, president of Allegheny Ludlum. "I read that there is a depression cartel now that six stainless steel companies in Japan set up to see what they could do for themselves." August Thyssen of West Germany reported a profitless first quarter in 1966. All German mills were in the same shape, said the Thyssen chairman.

"They're making no money," reported Harleston R. Wood, chairman of Alan Wood Steel Co. and a member of the United Nations European Economic Commission. "The European industry has not been profitable generally," said Rev. William Hogan, S.J., a cleric who has specialized in steel matters. "They're going broke," said a security analyst just back from a foreign tour. He cited a case in which one order had bounced around four nations and then wound up at a high-cost African mill.

So the steel industry had a beautiful illustration of what happened when pricing was done without regard to cost and mass production was imposed on a market. It might have been all right to hold fire sales 25 years ago when Japan was producing 8 million tons a year and western Europe less than 50 million tons. This just could not be done in 1965 when the capacity of Japan was 45 million tons and that of western Europe was 125 million tons.

Also instructive was the foreign reaction to price and trade problems. The initial dumping complaints in this country were pooh-poohed abroad. When they started having their own problems, the Common Market group quickly boosted external steel tariffs 50 per cent. "The western Europeans," said AISI, "at one point took the drastic step of placing embargoes and quotas on imports from Communist Bloc countries." In addition, foreign mills turned to their governments for help. German producers agitated for a subsidy on coal. The French government came through with low-interest financing for its steel companies.

Most important, however, there was a move to curb competition and eliminate competitors. "All the Japanese steel companies should be dissolved so as to establish two giant companies," said Shigeo Nagano, president, Fuji Iron & Steel Co. (Fuji later absorbed Tokai Iron & Steel Co., Ltd., to form an 11 million ton combine). In Germany, plans were made for coordinating the sales of 30 mills through four marketing outlets. In France, Usinor and Sollac agreed on a joint investment policy.

An item in the *Wall Street Journal* gives some idea of the approach to pricing in Europe. "The Community's steel industry operated at only 78 per cent of capacity last year (1966) and there was fierce—if illegal—price cutting in member nations. Price publication rules have also been tightened up by the coal-steel pool's executive commission to prevent this undercutting." The foreign reaction to unbridled competition was reversion to organizations that stifled competition. The American industry did seem to have found a middle ground. When the price bath was over abroad, there would be fewer steel companies and less competition.

So U. S. mills had been vindicated in their price policies. They had made a reasonably successful stand against government control and now they had an object lesson in the evils of auctioning off steel. The future seemed reasonably clear. But was it? Price-cutting had shown up the weakness and inefficiency of steel operations abroad. At this precise time, the American industry was coming on strong. Roger

Blough had said in 1962 that U. S. Steel was raising prices to become more competitive. This may not have been the happiest phrasing but it did have an element of truth. The mills finally got their price increase in 1963. Along with improved demand, this enabled them to raise spending from $1 billion that year to nearly $2 billion in 1964.

This rate was maintained in 1965 and 1966. It was maintained because the mills were making money. In 1965, the 10 largest U. S. mills spent just under $1.5 billion on new facilities and paid out nearly $400 million in dividends. These mills did practically no equity financing and, on a net basis, borrowed only $155 million. Most of the capital dollars came from a depreciation and earnings total of more than $1.8 billion. So at a time when the French mills were going to their government for money, American companies were making huge expenditures on a pay-as-you-go basis. And the spending wave was having an effect. By September of 1966, U. S. producers had taken stock of their own situations. They had read foreign financial statements. They had checked foreign plants. They had come to a conclusion.

"With the possible exception of the Japanese, I don't think anybody has substantially lower costs than ours," said Harleston R. Wood of Alan Wood Steel Co. Wood added that he was leaving Japan out only because of a lack of information. "I don't think anybody is doing any better than the U. S.—if as well," said Harry Lee Allen, vice-president and general manager of operations, Republic Steel Corp. Allen cited the report of one technical mission to Japan. "They were appalled by the number of people around operations," he said.

In any case, it had been pretty well established by 1966 that American steel mills were as efficient as any in the world. U. S. mills had put themselves in a position to make continuing improvements—at the rate of $2 billion a year. Price-cutting had shown up the high costs of foreign mills and left these mills strapped for capital dollars. In the opinion of many steel people, all this was academic. Relative costs didn't matter because foreign suppliers were selling without regard to cost and because foreign governments were providing all kinds of special aid.

Jones & Laughlin Steel Corp. people believed that the solution had to be political rather than commercial. By the time you unraveled all the rights and wrongs of dumping and tariffs, said Jones & Laughlin people, foreign mills would have captured 20 per cent of the American market. The only answer was immediate application of quotas. Others had their own remedies but this did seem to represent the mainstream of steel thinking in 1966. Commercial competition was not the answer to imports.

The mills had departed from this thinking in isolated cases. In 1961, they discontinued price schedules for reinforcing bars and began negotiating prices for individual jobs. The new method dropped the rebar price from 5.675¢ a ton in 1961 to an unofficial level of 4.50¢ a ton in 1963. It also dropped import tonnage—by 15 per cent in 1963. The question, however, was whether American mills were making any money at the lower prices. "Nothing plus nothing equals nothing," said one sales manager.

On April 29 of 1964, there was a second price move when U. S. Steel established a special wire rod class. The price for this rod was set $20 a ton under previous rates. The cut was aimed directly at imports. This attempt failed for a number of reasons. According to rod users, there was limited industry support for the lower prices when domestic demand started booming in the second half of 1964. Also, importers matched the cut. Finally, said fabricators, some of the domestic mills squeezed customers by lowering their own prices for finished wire products.

The rod and bar moves did not start a trend. Going into 1966, it was still the steel industry's position that imports could only be stopped by government action. Then on March 1, 1966, U. S. Steel announced that certain rod and nail prices would be "negotiated with the objective of competing with imports." At the time, this was regarded as simply a dodge to cover more important increases for plate. The discussion was all about whether U. S. Steel had surrendered to the government. Other mills quickly learned the price negotiation was by no means a token thing. "They're more than competitive in some areas," said a sales executive. "There's no reason for some of the cutting they're doing." "It's just a few dollars difference when you figure it on a delivered basis," said one converter. "We've placed some domestic orders."

U. S. Steel was indeed making some whopping cuts. Its new prices were running about $40 a ton under the levels of a few years ago. And it was getting orders. "There's no question U. S. Steel had picked up quite a bit of business," said Kurt Orban, a leading importer. "Particularly in the inland areas."

"It's worked as well as we thought," said Leslie B. Worthington, U. S. Steel president. "We've fought our way back into the market." It was also clear U. S. Steel had found a firm bottom with its prices. Foreign mills would have difficulty going lower. "You can cut prices just so much," said Kurt Orban. "A mill has to have some profit."

The question again was whether there was any profit left for domestic producers. U. S. Steel apparently thought so. Shortly after going to the new prices, it committed itself to a major rod mill on the East Coast. Others had their doubts. On March 2, the day after flexible nail prices were announced, Jones & Laughlin revealed it was closing its last remaining merchant wire facility—a nail mill at Aliquippa, Pennsylvania. "The mounting impact of foreign competition has put us in a position where we cannot see a sufficient volume of nails on a profitable basis to stay in that business," said William J. Stephens, Jones & Laughlin president.

On April 12, the problem of "brutal competition" in wire markets was discussed by Allison Maxwell of Pittsburgh Steel. "The erosion of selling prices for construction wire products has been as much as $40 a ton," said Maxwell. "We see nothing but trouble ahead." Shortly after, Pittsburgh Steel began phasing out its wire operations. Republic Steel was taking a hard look at its merchant wire line. There was general uncertainty. "The others just come around and want to know what U. S. Steel is doing," said one wire converter.

And that was the question: What was U. S. Steel doing? Top officials insisted there had been no broad policy change. The rod case had been special. Yet, it did appear that something new was afoot. Toward the end of March, Senator Vance Hartke (D., Ind.) was getting ready to announce hearings on a resolution dealing with steel imports.

On Monday, March 21, Commerce Secretary Connor called in John Roche, president of the American Iron & Steel Institute. Connor told Roche it was not a good time to be agitating against imports. Cited in this connection were the Vietnam crisis, the booming economy, and the international trade talks. Connor said a study made in this setting would not produce findings favorable to the steel industry. Roche relayed this message to steel leaders the next day. On March 23, the industry notified Senator Hartke it was withdrawing from the study project. The Senator blew his top. For years, steel people had been trying to get government help on imports. Now, he was trying and they were pulling the rug from under him.

It did seem a stunning reversal of form. Various explanations were offered. President Johnson was down on Senator Hartke, and the industry would be getting itself in the middle of a political fight. With domestic steel supply relatively tight, the hearings would simply provide small users and importers a platform for complaining about mill service. This point was stressed by John Roche. "The point of the study is not whether a particular user can get delivery in two months abroad and three months from U. S. mills. The issue is the impact of imports on the economy." In a boom atmosphere, said Roche, extraneous matters would have "beclouded the issue."

This explanation did not satisfy some steel people. The problem was long-range, said one official. It was ridiculous to delay a study because of immediate market conditions. It would take months to explore the question and more months to get remedies. The real problem, said this source, was that U. S. Steel had decided foreign competition must be met primarily by commercial means—without government intervention. Others agreed that a new pattern was showing up in statements and actions. "Some are saying this is primarily an economic battle," said a sales vice-president. "Apparently, that's the reason for U. S. Steel's new policy on wire."

On May 2, Roger Blough of U. S. Steel said this: "We are putting ever increasing emphasis on doing whatever must be done to beat the competition, whether domestic or foreign. . . . higher profits must come largely out of growth—growth in market competition and growth in efficiency of production." A few other steel leaders were making similar comments. "Our present efforts are simply to . . . counterbalance the effect of these costs and not to look for relief through price increases," said George Stinson, president of National Steel Corp., on April 27, 1966.

A U. S. Steel spokesman said people were taking Blough's words on efficiency out of context. They did run counter to other statements by Blough. They were decidedly at variance with most official expressions. "Certainly, we cannot face this problem (imports) as an industry head-on through economic means," said Robert E. Williams, president of Youngstown Sheet & Tube Co., on May 17. U. S. Steel executives insisted they were not making any sweeping changes in policy on imports or prices.

"We have always been competitive," said finance chairman Robert Tyson in September. Foreign producers did not represent normal competition and there could not be a normal response, he explained. In trying to compete abroad, he said, American mills faced "exorbitant fees." In home markets, there were dumping prices. Yet Tyson conceded that U. S. Steel had responded commercially to rebar and rod competition. "We have even had success in meeting something that goes beyond normal competition."

Then Tyson went on to say things that seemed to contradict his general statements. The import problem was not going to be solved by government edict alone, he said. "We have to be able to meet foreign competition through quality, through service, and through price." Tyson added that U. S. Steel was putting itself in a position from which it could make a full effort. "We have made substantial progress but we have not reached the end of the road yet." It was this situation that made the 7 per cent investment credit so important, he added.

Another U. S. Steel executive put it this way: "Our best facilities are now competitive with anything in the world. Within a few years, all our facilities will be." This executive, like Tyson, insisted that there had been no general policy shift. Imports had taken more than 47 per cent of the independent rod market and 50 per cent of the nail market. (Importers object that the rod percentage is inflated because it ignores the captive wire production of basic mills.)

In this situation, said the executive, there was really no choice on cutting prices or not cutting them; the market price had been established by imports. The only choice for a domestic producer was whether or not to stay in the

226

market. The same official also noted that the arithmetic of pricing had changed with the expansion of foreign volume. There was now the prospect that a price cut would produce significant added tonnage—up to 50 per cent more.

For many years, there had not been this positive incentive. Steel was the established metal. It had saturated markets. It was competing largely against itself. "Nobody gains in a price cut," steel veterans had said. This had once been true. There was just so much business. "You wouldn't go out and buy two cars if the price of steel were cut," Robert Tyson had said. Now the arithmetic had changed. The rod market was an extreme example of the volume immediately available with lower prices. In all steel markets and product lines, there were opportunities for significant gains.

Total imports in 1966 were 11 per cent of the American steel supply. Imports of hot-rolled sheet were over 20 per cent in individual months. Imports of cold-rolled sheet were well over 10 per cent at times. These losses were hitting at a time when steel technology was reaching a truly massive stage and steel profits were particularly sensitive to volume. All the big companies were putting in strip mills that could roll 3 to 5 million tons a year and cost about $100 million a piece. Wheeling Steel's deficit showed how the cost of this kind of equipment could drag a company down if it were not getting enough tonnage.

Without tonnage, a company's expenses could actually increase with a new mill. "We haven't come within dollars of our costs on the old line," said one steel engineer. "The payoff will come with added volume," said the president of the engineer's company. What were the prospects for this volume? "Imports are siphoning off the growth," said the executive.

Apart from imports, there was now much more significant competition from other metals. Stainless steel producers, who compete very directly with aluminum, had demonstrated that their market did have price-volume elasticity. By cutting prices 25 per cent, they had boosted volume 50 per cent. There had been some rough years for the stainless industry, but by 1966 leading producers were reporting record earnings, as well as record sales. Investors were taking a keen interest in the specialty end of the steel business. "We don't like big price increases," said one stainless man. "If we can reduce total cost 15 per cent, we can penetrate markets," said H. F. Peters, director of marketing, Crucible Steel Co. of America.

Peters noted that, in recent years, new industries had grown up around other metals. In many of these industries, he said, fabricators had no knowledge of the properties of stainless steel. All this added up to some tough decisions for steel people. For the first time in 50 years, they faced a situation in which added volume was available if the price was right. They needed this volume for their big machines. They knew now they were as efficient as foreign mills and in much sounder financial condition.

At the same time, they could see the results of all-out price aggression. "Cost is the least significant factor in pricing," said Robert Morris, president of Wheeling Steel Corp. Ultimately, said Morris, price was set by relative values in the market. In line with this thinking, Wheeling adopted a policy of guaranteeing customers against price increases for set periods. The new policy did get business; Wheeling's shipments rose in 1966 when total industry shipments dropped. But over the first 9 months of the year, Wheeling reported a loss of $12 million. Overseas, steel mills were going broke trying to get volume through prices.

In this situation, it was possibly no wonder steel statements were contradictory. "They're not kidding you," said a middle manager of U. S. Steel. "We don't know what our policy should be." That, in itself, was something. For years, cost had been the base and the bible. At that particular

228

moment, in late 1966, it appeared that U. S. Steel was at least leaning toward a new emphasis on world competition as the prime controlling factor.

If this budding deviation ever was an actuality, it was snuffed out by another rush of events. In September, the Administration took away the 7 per cent investment credit. Coming just as a few steel people were saying the industry could spend its way to a competitive position, the suspension was a decisive move. Abroad, governments were extending helping hands to steel companies. The American industry was getting socked with a new tax burden and one that struck directly at the power to modernize. At the same time domestic demand was dropping. Shipments, which were over 8 million tons in March, had dropped to around 7 million by November and December.

And imports were not dropping. Until the St. Lawrence Seaway closed in December, foreign tonnage remained close to 1 million tons a month. Steel men noted what the American Iron & Steel Institute later described as foreign as "measures to stabilize domestic markets and incidentally provide a base for low-price exports. . . ."

All this brought a closing of ranks and a hardening of thoughts. Steel mills put through price hikes for stainless steel, tool steel, and finally pipe products. Standard pipe was a big import item. The increase meant domestic mills were closing the door very firmly on the idea of meeting import prices. Also rejected, apparently, was the doctrine of peaceful coexistence with government. Protests from Gardner Ackley on price moves were shrugged off very casually. The industry had had enough of government meddling in its affairs.

But while this was happening, the industry was asking the government to meddle. On December 8, a top-level steel delegation visited a top administration team. The session was arranged on the initiative of the industry. "Our message is not getting through to the policy makers," steel management had been told. Arrangements were made to meet with Gardner Ackley; Christian Herter, top tariff negotiator; and representatives of the State, Labor, Treasury, and Commerce Departments.

Various steel problems were covered by L. B. Worthington, president, U. S. Steel; E. F. Martin, chairman, Bethlehem Steel; T. F. Patton, chairman, Republic Steel; and T. S. Fitch, president of Washington Steel Corp., a stainless sheet producer. The topic of imports was assigned to C. M. Beeghly, chairman of Jones & Laughlin. This was of interest because Beeghly was among the more adamant protectionists in the steel industry. The meeting produced no specific moves but steel people were mildly encouraged by their reception. "They were very attentive and polite," said one participant. "Gardner Ackley asked the same questions you would expect him to ask. The man for the State Department sat there and frowned."

A second Washington session—with congressional leaders—was scheduled for February 8. Considerably before this date, reports began to circulate about a new steel program for combating imports. No details were available as specialists hacked out recommendations, but it was clear the aspirations of any free traders were being swallowed. "It's not quotas," said one official, "but it's something almost as bad."

Basic thinking was keynoted by Leslie B. Worthington, U. S. Steel president. "There is a point—and I think that point has arrived—when this export-import problem of the steel industry must be recognized in the offices of government."

On February 8, the industry formally unveiled its package at a breakfast for congressional leaders. That particular morning, Washington was digging out of a blizzard that
230

had closed National Airport and made all movement difficult. This kind of weather is unusual for Washington yet a year earlier, when the industry was staging its first congressional breakfast, another freak blizzard hit and attendance at the meeting was reduced.

The point is, steel leaders are unlucky. Some gypsy curse seems to make for unhappy accidents and unfortunate coincidence. When they begin agitating against Japanese imports, the Vietnam fighting heats up and makes friendship with Japan essential. When they seem to be solving labor problems, the steel union has its first political fight. When U. S. Steel is dedicating a new office building, balmy weather suddenly turns to a drizzle and then snow. Thus, the steel plea for protection was being made with snow on the streets and the world situation in the worst possible state for anyone to seek trade protection.

Nevertheless, Leslie B. Worthington and the other steel leaders made a powerful plea. Since 1955, said Worthington, "world production of raw steel had increased from 207 million tons to 501 million tons. Moreover, it appears that at least 75 million additional tons could have been produced had there been a market for this steel." Because of excess capacity, producers had increased exports—from 23 million tons in 1955 to 51 million tons in 1965. "And no longer does this steel flow principally from the industrialized nations to the less developed countries," said Worthington. "Twenty per cent of it comes into the United States, so that this nation—which is the world's largest producer of steel—has become paradoxically the world's largest importer of steel."

In a fuller development of the subject, steel men pointed out that this movement was contrary to underlying principles of the Trade Expansion Act and the GATT talks. The idea had been to eliminate tariffs and permit trade to take its normal, natural course. The nations best situated for production of certain items would supply these items to others and buy goods that others could do a better job on.

The fallacy of this theory was being demonstrated said steel people. The Japanese were buying coal in West Virginia and scrap in Detroit. The materials were shipped to Japan, used to make steel, and the finished product was being shipped back to Detroit and Chicago. Also dislocating things was the desire of new nations to build steel mills as prestige items. For the most part, these nations lacked the markets to support large steel operations. When they went ahead with their own mills, they cut off natural export markets for others and created further surpluses for the world market.

The American industry, said Worthington, was doing all it could to make itself competitive. ". . . we are now spending considerably in excess of $100 million a year on research." (Steel sales were over $17 billion in 1965; the industry has been criticized for the small percentage of its revenue that goes to research.) Worthington noted that the industry had put $13 billion into capital equipment over the previous 10 years and was currently spending at the rate of $2 billion a year.

Why hadn't this effort enabled the mills to check imports? Well, for one thing, the Japanese also had modern equipment. Their industry had been largely rebuilt since the war. They were every bit as good as American steelmakers. "There is little to choose between the two as to technology, productivity, labor supply, skills, and climate," said Worthington. This country had a slight edge on raw materials and transportation, but the only real difference was in labor rates. "Employment costs in the Japanese steel industry are less than one-third as much as they are in the United States. . . . The net result is that the Japanese mills have an advantage of from $30 to $35 a ton in employment costs alone." He said the Japs also had lower capital costs. "Faced by that kind of a cost disadvantage, American producers have little chance of competing on a basis of price and must rely on quality, service, and innovation."

Earlier, Robert Tyson had included price, along with quality and service, as an area of competition. Also earlier, steel people had talked less about wages as the prime problem. There seemed to be growing confidence that wage differentials could be overcome and U. S. mills could match the costs of foreign producers. Now, there was a flat, official statement to the contrary. "American producers have little chance of competing on the basis of price," said Worthington. The industry moved back 5 years and presented itself as helpless and hopeless.

Worthington then went on to discuss other aspects of the problem. Foreign mills were under pressure to maintain full employment. They were encouraged and aided by their governments in the unloading of surplus tonnage on other markets. They were subsidized in their exports and sheltered from imports. "Foreign governments use their steel industries as instruments of national policy . . ." said Worthington. There seems to be no question that steel has been used for international bartering. It is a relatively simple and standardized product. As opposed to complex manufactured items, it presents no problem on service or replacement parts.

In addition, foreign planners have followed a development sequence that placed steel production ahead of metalworking activity. Proceeding from basic raw materials through basic industries, they tended to arrive at end products last. This was particularly true of the new nations, but in Europe too there was a tendency to build without regard to existing markets. In any case, said Worthington, foreign nations were determined to export steel no matter what. America had become the prime target because of the size of its market and because "it is also the most open and easily accessible in the world." A low 6 per cent tariff was the "only barrier."

On the other hand, American steel exports faced tariffs that "can be more than double the U. S. duty. In addition there were nontariff barriers "which may include border taxes, surcharges, import licenses, penalties, fees, and so-called equalization taxes. . . . So the United States market is thus being used by foreign mills as a kind of bargain basement in which to dispose of their surplus production."

"Gentlemen," concluded Worthington, "there is a point —and I believe that point has been reached—where there is a limit to what we can do and still maintain the financial soundness that steel or any other industry cannot and must not jeopardize." The import problem "must be recognized in the offices of government. . . ." Worthington then recommended that Congress apply a special levy to steel and pig iron imports "so as to narrow the price differential and create a climate of more equitable competition between domestic and foreign producers. . . ."

Worthington did not explain exactly what was meant by a temporary levy. Most news accounts simply said the steel industry wanted higher tariffs. Actually, the industry had in mind something more drastic than a conventional percentage tariff. Steel specialists had drawn up a schedule of price differentials on all major products at all locations. For example, they had listed the spread between domestic and imported reinforcing steel in Florida. The idea was to apply an import tax large enough to equalize the two prices.

"It's international price-fixing," said one official blandly. He explained that the tax would never actually be collected. Foreign mills would avoid it by raising their prices to the American level. And that, said the steel official, would eliminate 95 per cent of the import tonnage. These refinements were missed in news stories but the basic thought did come through: American steelmakers were seeking protection from foreign steelmakers.

The general reaction was predictable. "It is difficult to conceive of any action that could embarrass the American representative (in GATT talks) more than suddenly slamming the door on imported steel," said the *Wall Street Journal* on February 14. ". . . the U. S. stands to gain more from freer trade than other countries . . . the steel industry in its protected domestic market would be more likely in time to become even less capable of competing in international market . . . tariff increases are not only debilitating subsidies to special interest groups but hidden taxes on consumers."

The *Journal* threw in an uninformed dig to the effect that Bethlehem Steel was doing all right in its earnings. If U. S. Steel would hustle a little more, maybe it would not need protection. The suggestion was that U. S. Steel was dragging the rest of the industry along on a project designed to cover its own competitive shortcomings. Actually, the truth was just the opposite. U. S. Steel had been leaning toward a free trade position. The loudest demands for protection had come from other mills.

The *Journal* editorial made no attempt to examine the arguments of the steel companies. It swept these aside with the statement that free trade was benefiting this country. The inference was that any industry seeking protection was probably backward and would become worse if sheltered. The first part of this thesis was probably true. The United States had a favorable trade balance of $4 to $5 billion. We are the only nation that has consistently had a trade surplus for the past 50 years. For the standpoint of broad interest, it made no sense for us to adopt protectionist measures that might invite retaliation. It was this question of broad interest that had stymied all steel demands for government action against imports.

Closely related was the diplomatic question. Steel import curbs would produce a "terrible" reaction in Japan, said Edwin O. Reischauer, former Ambassador to Japan. Japan depended on this country for 30 per cent of its export trade, said Dr. Reischauer. The Japanese were extremely touchy on the subject of protectionism, and they were particularly edgy at this particular time because of Vietnam. The friendship of Japan was "absolutely vital to our position in that part of the world," said Dr. Reischauer. So the steel people were going against the tide in the attempts to seal themselves off.

That doesn't mean they did not have a legitimate problem. It was all very good to talk about modernizing but the steel companies had been modernizing. Government studies showed that they were two or three times more productive than European mills. Likewise, it was fine to talk about healthy competition, but what should you do when less efficient competitors were selling steel at prices below your costs?

American steel mills earned $12 to $14 a ton in 1966, said William J. Stephens, president of Jones & Laughlin. "The difference between domestic prices and foreign import prices is more than double that figure," said Stephens. He rattled off tariff and freight differentials. German plate could enter this country for a charge of $25. For American plate going into Germany, the charge was $43.

Steel people argued that you couldn't brush aside those numbers with talk about invigorating competition. But deep down, there was still the nagging question: Why steel? Why should this one industry be having trouble when so many others were prospering in the world market?

Part of the answer was that not all industries were doing

well. Imports had wiped out half the domestic glass tableware industry. Foreign producers had taken over 25 per cent of the sheet glass market. The textile people had been hard hit.

Nevertheless, there were obviously more gainers than losers. One characteristic of the gainers is that they have put down roots abroad. International Business Machines Corp. has nearly $1 billion in foreign assets. In 1966, foreign markets produced more than one-third of IBM's sales. General Electric Co. has something like 60,000 people in foreign operations. The auto companies have been producing abroad for years. Machine-tool builders were locating plants in Europe.

One advantage an international structure gives a company is a hedge against imports. When the oil companies were trying to raise prices in February of 1967, the Administration threatened to increase crude oil imports by 30,000 barrels a day. This brought protests from oil people but also a few chuckles. The major U. S. oil companies, it was noted, were the owners and importers of foreign oil. They might be hurt by the price disruption, but they were in a pretty good position to let the chips fall where they may.

This is true in other lines. The third largest supplier of cash registers in this country is a Swedish company. The Company is owned by Litton Industries. A leading machine-tool builder offers prospects two prices—one for a machine built in this country and the other for the same unit put together in the company's European plant. By and large, however, companies are not building plants abroad to compete with their own plants in this country. The big advantage of foreign production is that it gives a company entree overseas. You're not an outsider or an "in-and-outer." You have the ties and the personnel that establish you as a native. IBM notes that its French and German plants are contributing to the export sales of these countries. IBM also

237

explains that its foreign operations are largely manned by foreigners. The Americans could be brought home "in one planeload."

It has been pretty well established that a company must move abroad—physically and financially—in order to sell abroad. The American steel companies have never made this move. With the exception of Armco Steel, the major companies have never gone outside this country except for raw materials. By 1967, this picture was changing. U. S. Steel was participating in a 1-million-ton expansion of Altos Hornos—a Spanish mill. There were reports of American interest in a big Brazilian complex. There was a Greek mill in the works and a second Spanish operation.

A few ventures had started earlier. Allegheny Ludlum had gone in on a Belgian stainless sheet mill. Crucible Steel had an Italian specialty plant. Pittsburgh Steel Co. and Armco had joined in a Belgian strip mill. All these were fairly limited operations. Now, some king-sized facilities were being discussed. The difficulty was that there was already too much steel abroad. More important, however, there was too much price-cutting. American steel men knew how to make money at 80 per cent of capacity, but they weren't keen on this business of forgoing profits altogether.

According to one steel official, the interest in foreign investment was one of the reasons for the proposed levy on import. The levy would force foreign mills to raise prices. They would get less business but they'd probably be better off profitwise. And a profit improvement, he said, would make it more attractive for an American mill to build a plant in Japan. This last comment may have been facetious but it was true that U. S. mills were checking into the question of foreign plants. It was all very confusing. The steel people were talking about a world steel glut and about protection from foreign competition. At the same time, they were looking into foreign investments.

238

Also at the same time, the mills were talking about price stability. In March of 1967, Pittsburgh Steel Co. said there was little prospect of price relief during the year. Jones & Laughlin noted a cost-price squeeze in its annual report but made no mention of price increases. Other major mills stuck to noncommittal statements about prices. This was unusual because the steel companies had always devoted large portions of their shareholders' reports to the inadequacy of prices. Moreover, reports from markets suggested that any price movement might be down rather than up. Steel shipments had dropped from 8.3 million tons in March of 1966 to 6.5 million tons by February of 1967. Declining demand had brought with it an intensifying of competitive pressures. Steel prices, which had always stood firm in fair weather or foul, were under serious attack by purchasing agents. "This is going to be a real challenge," said one steel official.

Not helping matters was the fact that while demand was dropping, imports were rising. In the first 2 months of 1967, foreign shipments rose by more than 300,000 tons over the same period of 1966. Users of steel were making sure the mills did not forget about the foreign threat. By hints, warnings, and actual import orders, purchasing agents hammered away at domestic prices. So it appeared that a new price policy was being forced on the industry. Whether they liked it or not, the mills were going to be drawn into world competition.

That was the way it looked, but key steel executives counseled otherwise. "Prices aren't going down," they said. "They're going up." The mills were not going to let imports set their prices. They were not going to let climbing costs eat away profits. "There will be a continuation of last year," said this executive. Prices would be increased one by one, over a period of time.

That was the way things stood in early 1967. Steel men

were seeking governmental protection. They were talking about price stability and they were talking about price increases. They were facing a serious market challenge. They were thinking about global operations. "Nations will find isolation of any kind unbearable," said Roger Blough in 1965.

It was clear the last word had not come. The story on steel wages and prices is not over. Unfortunately, this is a story that doesn't seem to have any end. Just when it seems that something will be settled, there is a new twist and a whole new train of events. Possibly, the one general conclusion in 1967 was that nothing was certain in the steel wage-price picture. There were no longer any automatic reactions or firm guidelines. Everything was subject to challenge and change.